A PHOTOGRAPHIC GUIDE TO

BIRDS
OF
ISRAEL
AND THE MIDDLE EAST

DAVID M. COTTRIDGE
and RICHARD PORTER

GW00578179

First published in 2000 by
New Holland Publishers (UK) Ltd
London • Cape Town • Sydney • Auckland

24 Nutford Place   80 McKenzie Street
London W1H 6DQ   Cape Town 8001
United Kingdom   South Africa

14 Aquatic Drive   218 Lake Road
Frenchs Forest, NSW 2086   Northcote, Auckland
Australia   New Zealand

ISBN 1 85974 508 3

Publishing Manager/Commissioning Editor: Jo Hemmings
Editor: David Christie
Assistant Editor: Michaella Standen
Design and cartography: D & N Publishing, Hungerford, Berkshire
Production Controller: Joan Woodroffe

Reproduction by Modern Age Repro House Limited, Hong Kong
Printed and bound in Malaysia by Times Offset (M) Sdn Bhd

10 9 8 7 6 5 4 3 2 1

Front cover photograph: Black-headed Bunting (David M. Cottridge)
Title page photograph: Palestine Sunbird (David M. Cottridge)

Contents

Introduction. 4

How to use this book 5

The photographs 5

The species descriptions 5

Glossary. 6

Identifying birds. 6

Key to corner tabs 7

Going birdwatching 9

Where to watch birds in Israel 9

Map of Israel and the Middle East . . 10–11

Useful addresses. 13

Species descriptions 14

Further reading 140

Index 141

Introduction

For birds, Israel is by far the most studied country in the Middle East. Not only does it have the highest number of species recorded (over 510), but a number of these have been studied in depth. The migration research, particularly on birds of prey, is probably the best of any country in the world, and the book *The Birds of Israel*, by Hadoram Shirihai, published in 1996, is regarded by many as the most outstanding account of the birds of any single country.

In addition, Israel has a very active bird and wildlife conservation programme. The Society for the Protection of Nature in Israel (SPNI) and the government's Nature Reserves Authority (NRA) are models of their kind, and these bodies, through research, the establishment of nature reserves and, in particular, the education of young people, have spearheaded the conservation movement in the Middle East. This is especially important, as Israel is a small country with a growing population, and human pressure for land and water – in one sense, wildlife versus people – should not be underestimated.

This book covers 252 species of bird found in Israel. Choosing these from the 511 that have been recorded has not been easy, but we have concentrated on those that are most familiar (particularly the desert specialities), are most likely to be seen by the birdwatching tourist or, although rare, cannot be left out as they are important 'Israeli birds'. In this respect, it should be noted that Israel is one of the countries in Europe and the Middle East most visited by birdwatchers who want to see birds that are special to the region, which are difficult to see elsewhere or which might turn up as vagrants at times of migration. Eilat, for example, along with its environs on the Gulf of Aqaba, is one of the most famous places in the world for witnessing the spectacle of bird migration, with a strong dash of the unexpected.

Many of the birds included in this book are residents in Israel. These are joined in spring by summer visitors, birds that have spent the winter in Africa and which return to breed in Israel in the summer. The total number of regular breeding species – residents and summer visitors combined – is over 170. Then, there are those birds that breed to the north in Europe and Asia and which, as the daylength shortens, migrate south to winter, often in large numbers, in Israel and the Middle East. In addition, there are the numerous passage migrants which fly between their breeding grounds to the north and wintering grounds to the south; for many of them, Israel is a fertile corridor for use in spring and autumn to refuel and rest on what can often be a hazardous journey. Over 120 species regularly migrate through Israel.

Finally, there are the rarities, usually referred to as vagrants or accidentals, which for many birdwatchers are the greatest fascination, simply because their occurrence is unpredictable. Israel has more than its fair share of this large group, which has grown considerably in number with the increasing intensity of birding activity. We have included only a few Israel rarities but, if your interest in birds is fired by this book, we are sure that you will want to know more about those which have occurred and how to identify them.

How to use this book

The birds in this book are presented in what is known as systematic order. This is scientific jargon which means that, in very broad terms, the sequence progresses from the most ancient species to the most recently evolved – according to our current state of knowledge. The English names of birds have always given rise to confusion, for rarely do any two books agree on this matter. In this book, we have adopted those used in the *Field Guide to the Birds of the Middle East*, published by T & AD Poyser in 1996.

The photographs

Each species in this book is accompanied by at least one colour photograph. For many species the plumages of the male and the female are identical, and identification from the photograph should present no problem. For others, however, males and females differ. In such cases, we have usually depicted the male but described the female in the text. Immature birds can present a problem to the beginner, and often to the expert as well. Some immatures can be quite different from both male and female adults, being generally drabber, with fewer diagnostic features. Again, we have tried to cover these in the text, where space has permitted.

Some species also have a different plumage in winter from that in summer, the winter dress normally lacking the colour and finery of that when breeding. Here, we have generally used photographs of the plumage most likely to be seen in Israel.

The species descriptions

The descriptions provide additional information to the photograph to help with identification.

Common name. In all cases, we have used the name in *Field Guide to the Birds of the Middle East*.

Scientific name. Each species has a Latin-based scientific name, recognized throughout the world. There have been some changes in recent years, but here we have again followed the *Field Guide*.

Length. After the scientific name, the approximate length in centimetres, from bill tip to end of tail, is given.

Range and status. Each species account includes a statement on the bird's status in Israel (resident, summer visitor, passage migrant, winter visitor or vagrant). There is also a brief mention of the species' range in the Middle East, to help put the Israel status into context. In this respect, the Middle East is taken to cover the whole of Arabia to the Mediterranean coast, and north to include Turkey and Cyprus.

Glossary

coverts The small feathers at base of quill feathers forming main flight surfaces of wing and tail
endemic Indigenous species restricted to a particular area
eyebrow Contrasting line above eye (supercilium)
eye-stripe Contrasting line through eye
flank Side of the body
gregarious Frequently occurring in groups
migrant Non-resident traveller
necklace A line of markings around front of neck
orbital ring Unfeathered bare ring around eye
primaries The main outer flight feathers (show as longest part of folded wing)
race Another name for subspecies
resident Remaining in a local area throughout year
roost Resting or sleeping place
secondaries The inner flight feathers on rear half of wing
subspecies A population which is morphologically different from other populations of same species
supercilium A stripe above eye (eyebrow)
terminal At the end or tip
underparts Undersurface of body from throat to undertail-coverts
undertail-coverts Small feathers below tail covering bases of tail feathers
underwing-coverts Small underwing feathers covering bases of primaries and secondaries
upperparts Upper surface of body
vent Area around anus, including undertail-coverts
wingbar A visible line of colour at tips of wing-coverts
wing-coverts Small feathers on wing covering bases of primaries and secondaries

Identifying birds

Identifying birds can often be frustrating for the beginner, and sometimes for the experienced observer, too. This also can be part of the fun of birdwatching: pitting your skills of observation against a creature that refuses to show itself clearly or, when it does, reveals only a back view as it flies away. Most of the birds in this book should be fairly easy to identify, provided a reasonable view is obtained. If you fail to put a name to a bird, how-

Key to corner tabs

Ostriches & grebes

Shearwaters to pelicans

Herons, egrets & storks

Ducks & geese

Raptors

Gamebirds

Rails to bustards

Waders

Gulls & terns

Sandgrouse, pigeons & doves

Cuckoos

Owls & nightjars

Swifts

Kingfishers

Bee-eaters, rollers & hoopoe

Woodpeckers

Larks

Swallows

Pipits & wagtails

Bulbuls & hypocolius

Dunnocks, robins & chats

Thrushes

Warblers

Flycatchers & babblers

Tits & nuthatches

Sunbirds & orioles

Shrikes

Jays & crows

Starlings

Sparrows, finches & buntings

ever, make a note of what you saw and you will be a step nearer to identifying the species the next time you happen across it.

Your skills as a birdwatcher will improve as you gain experience. To assist this process, you should concentrate on the following aspects.

1. Size. It is not easy to gauge size, and it is therefore most helpful to try to compare the bird in question with a known species. 'Larger than a sparrow', 'smaller than a crow' or simply 'a very large, tall bird' are all very useful starting points for a correct identification.

2. Shape. Birds of particular families have a distinctive shape. Herons and egrets, for example, are rather large, with long neck and legs; and all birds of prey have a hooked bill, while buzzards and eagles also have broad wings. In addition to size, it is especially important to note the shape of the bill and the length of the legs. Some features will often immediately enable an identification to be made, such as the presence of a crest or tail-streamers.

3. Colour. A knowledge of feather-tracts is the basis for describing a bird's plumage, and noting the colour pattern accurately is essential for making a correct identification. The stylized drawing of a typical bunting shows these parts of a bird's plumage clearly, and if you want to progress in the skills of bird identification it is vital that you learn them. No matter how poor an artist you are, make a sketch of any bird that you cannot identify and use this stylized drawing to note the colours and markings.

4. Behaviour. Watch the way a bird feeds: does it search for insects, or is it a fruit- or seed-eater?

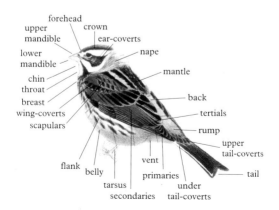

Is it tree- or ground-dwelling? Does it fly fast or slowly? Is it found in flocks? These are all aspects that can assist greatly with identification.

5. Habitat. Every species of bird is adapted to live in a particular habitat, and this is an important clue to its identity. Most species of wader, for example, are found on the shores of wetlands, including the sea, where they feed on invertebrates that live in the mud. Larks generally inhabit flat, open areas, some species in deserts and others in cultivated fields.

6. Voice. Some songs and calls are very distinctive and, once heard, are never forgotten. Most, however, can be quite subtle, or similar among several species. While listening to tapes will help, there is no substitute for learning a bird's voice in the field.

Going birdwatching

Although it is possible to watch birds without any equipment, binoculars will add greatly to your enjoyment. Later on, you may wish to purchase a telescope. These items of optical equipment can be very expensive, and it is inadvisable to rush into making a purchase until you are sure of what would be best suited to your needs. Before you make a decision, the first step is to test binoculars and telescopes extensively, ideally by seeing what your local birdwatchers are using and asking to try them out.

There are a few simple guidelines, however. Never buy a binocular with a magnification of more than ×10, as it will be difficult to hold steady; ideally, the magnification should be between ×7 and ×10. The size of the object lens should not be less than 30 or the light-gathering power will be poor. Most birdwatchers use 8 × 30, 8 × 40 or 10 × 40. Always consider the weight, as a heavy pair of binoculars can cause you neck-ache and arm-ache.

So far as telescopes are concerned, again watch to see what other birdwatchers are using and ask to look through them. Remember that a sturdy tripod is important, as a flimsy one will move easily in the slightest breeze and this will annoy you intensely.

Where to watch birds in Israel

There are numerous places to watch birds in Israel, which, despite its small size, has one of the richest avifaunas in the Middle East. The following are some of the special places to visit, but there are many more, as you will soon discover for yourself if you travel widely. Useful information on sites can be found in *Important Bird Areas in the Middle East* (details under 'Further reading', page 140). Further information on

Black Sea

TURKEY
● Ankara

R. Tigris

R. Euphrates

CYPRUS

SYRIA

LEBANON

Mediterranean
Sea

Beirut ●

● Damascus

IRAC

ISRAEL

WEST BANK

Jerusalem ●

● Amman

GAZA

JORDAN

ISRAEL

Mediterranean
Sea

Mt
Hermon ▲

Hula
Reserve

⑦ ⑧

⑥

Haifa ●

⑤

R. Jordan

Tel Aviv ●

WEST
BANK

Jerusalem ●

④

GAZA ●

● Be'er
Sheva

③

② ●

N
↑

① Eilat

KEY TO SITES

① Eilat
② The Arava Valley
③ The Negev Desert
④ The Dead Sea
⑤ Ma'agan Mikhael
⑥ Lake Tiberias
⑦ The Hula
⑧ Mount Hermon and
   the Golan Heights

Area not covered
by book

birdwatching can be obtained by contacting the Society for the Protection of Nature in Israel, 4 Hashfela Street, Tel Aviv 66183, Israel. In addition, the Ornithological Society of the Middle East publishes a journal, *Sandgrouse*, which contains many useful articles on Israel and the Middle East generally. Its address is OSME, c/o The Lodge, Sandy, Bedfordshire, SG19 2DL, U.K.

1. Eilat. This is probably the best place to watch birds in Israel in spring and autumn, as it is a stopping-off point for migrants to rest and feed on their north–south migrations. The habitats include the sea, beaches, lagoons, palm groves, fields, deserts and neighbouring mountains. The unexpected can turn up at any time, and Eilat has earned the reputation of being the best place in the Middle East to see rare birds and raptor migration.

2. The Arava Valley. This is the northern extension of the African Rift Valley and it runs between Eilat and the Dead Sea. It is a good area for seeing larks, Arabian Warbler and Arabian Babbler. Probably the best places to stop off and walk are at Hazeva and Yotvata.

3. The Negev Desert. This stone-and-sand desert to the south of Be'er Sheva is a good area for some of the desert specialities, such as Houbara Bustard, Cream-coloured Courser, sandgrouse, Hoopoe Lark, and various wheatears. The road to Nizzana will take you through some of the best habitats.

4. The Dead Sea. The edge of the Dead Sea, at Ein Gedi, is the best place in Israel to see Hume's Tawny Owl. Look for it at night, feeding on moths attracted by the spotlights around the field school. Many typical birds of Israel will be found on the cliffs along the edge of the Dead Sea, including Tristram's Grackle, Blackstart, White-crowned Black Wheatear and Scrub Warbler. In April, there is an impressive northerly migration of raptors, especially Lesser Spotted Eagles.

5. Ma'agan Mikhael. This is a complex of fish ponds on the Mediterranean coast which attracts a wealth of herons, wildfowl, waders and gulls – in winter, look for Great Black-headed Gulls. All three species of kingfisher that occur in Israel can be found here.

6. Lake Tiberias. The Sea of Galilee, as it will be known to many, holds surprisingly few birds, although it can be good for ducks and grebes in winter. The surrounding hills are well worth visiting for vultures, eagles, rock thrushes and wheatears.

7. The Hula. This impressive wetland is now a nature reserve run by the Nature Reserves Authority. It is part of a once much more extensive marsh which was drained for agriculture; there is now a management plan to reverse this and to return the area to its full former glory. The reserve is open to the public, and there are viewing platforms and hides. The Hula can be good at any time of the year, but note especially its migrant White Pelicans and wintering birds of prey. The threatened Marbled Teal breeds, and there are always herons and other waterfowl present.

8. Mount Hermon and the Golan Heights. These localities have a heavy military presence, as they are close to Israel's northern border. You are advised to seek permission to bird-watch, and in any event you should not stray from the road. There is a good population of birds of prey, as well as mountain species which are difficult to see elsewhere in Israel. The latter include Black Redstart, Sombre Tit, Western Rock Nuthatch, Syrian Serin and Rock Bunting. In winter Radde's Accentors occur, but they are not common.

Useful addresses

Society for the Protection of Nature in Israel (SPNI)
4 Hashfela Street, Tel Aviv 66183, Israel
Tel: 972 3 6388666
Fax: 972 3 6877695

Israel Ornithological Centre (IOC)
Atidim Industrial Park, PO Box 58020, Tel Aviv 61580, Israel
Tel: 972 3 6449622
Fax: 972 3 6449625

International Birding Centre at Eilat
PO Box 774, Eilat 77806, Israel
Tel: 972 7 6335339
Fax: 972 7 6335319

Ornithological Society of the Middle East (OSME)
c/o Royal Society for the Protection of Birds (RSPB)
The Lodge, Sandy, Bedfordshire, SG19 2DL, UK

Ostrich *Struthio camelus* 210cm

There is little point in describing the Ostrich, the largest bird in the world. In the Middle East, the species became extinct in the 1930s as a result of hunting with motor vehicles and firearms, and all that remains of these fine birds in their wild state in the region is eggshell fragments from the deserts. In 1973, a reintroduction programme was started in Israel, by raising birds in captivity for release into the wild. The captive stock can be seen in large enclosures at Hai Bar.

Great Crested Grebe *Podiceps cristatus* 50cm

The largest grebe, with characteristic chestnut and black head plumes in summer – important adornments in head-shaking display. In winter these are lost, and it is then dark grey above, with a black crown, and white below – especially noticeable on the neck. The long pinkish bill, white foreneck and large size separate it from all other grebes. Found on freshwater lakes, and also on coastal waters in winter, often in large flocks. A winter visitor to Israel from breeding grounds to the north; winters also in the Arabian Gulf and south to Egypt.

Black-necked Grebe *Podiceps nigricollis* 30cm

A small grebe which, in summer plumage, has an all-black neck and upperparts with fan-shaped yellow ear-tufts. These are lost in winter, when it is a basically black and white bird with white fore-neck, small upturned black bill and ruby-red eye. When breeding, occurs in small colonies on well-vegetated lakes, but in winter congregations of several hundred can frequently be seen on lakes and in coastal waters. A winter visitor to Israel in small numbers.

Cory's Shearwater *Calonectris diomedea* 46cm

Richard Porter

A large shearwater with greyish-brown upperparts and white underparts, lacking distinctive markings other than a yellow bill. Birds seen off the Mediterranean coast are likely to be in flight, which is relaxed, with slow wingbeats alternating with long arching glides; those seen in the Gulf of Eilat may well be in small, rather inactive groups sitting on the water for much of the time. This maritime species occurs in the east Mediterranean throughout the year, and is now a regular visitor to the Gulf of Eilat; elsewhere in the Middle East it is rare.

Mediterranean Shearwater *Puffinus yelkouan* 33cm
(wing 80cm)

One of the best places to see this seabird is Istanbul in Turkey, where for many months of the year thousands pass up and down the Bosphorus. It is easily told by its 'black and white' plumage, long wings, and rapid flight with occasional short glides just a few centimetres above the waves. In good light, the upperparts can be seen to be brown. In Israel, it is best seen along the Mediterranean coast, especially in autumn and winter, when birds wander from their Aegean breeding area.

Red-billed Tropicbird *Phaethon aethereus* 50cm (plus 50cm tail)

A white seabird with long white tail-streamers, black eye-stripe, black wingtips and all-red bill. Rather fast flight, well above the water, in which glides are interspersed with quick wingbeats. Usually seen singly or in pairs. A maritime species that breeds on rocky cliffs and islands. Resident in the Red Sea (especially off coast of Egypt), the coast of southern Arabia and the Arabian Gulf; wanderers have occurred occasionally off Eilat.

16

Brown Booby *Sula leucogaster* 70cm (wing 140cm)

Richard Porter

A large, Gannet-like seabird with chocolate-brown upperparts and head, and white underparts. The powerful creamy-yellow bill, with which it catches fish from a plunge-dive, can be seen at a distance contrasting with the brown head and neck. Juveniles are easily told by the brownish wash to the white underparts. Occurs widely in the Red Sea, and is a regular visitor to the Gulf of Eilat.

Pygmy Cormorant *Phalacrocorax pygmeus* 48cm

The smallest cormorant to occur in the Middle East, and with a rather short neck, stubby bill and long tail. In flight has noticably faster wingbeats than its larger cousin. In the breeding season, the glossy black plumage is inconspicuously spotted white. Its head and neck are bronzy brown in colour. Frequents large freshwater lakes with reedbeds and scattered trees and bushes, in which it nests. Breeds in scattered colonies in Turkey and on the Iraq marshes, often with Great Cormorants (*Phalacrocorax carbo*) and herons; disperses locally in winter, reaching northern Israel, especially the Hula, where flocks of several dozen have been recorded.

J. Lawton Roberts; Windrush Photos

17

White Pelican *Pelecanus onocrotalus* 160cm

(Above) adult; (below) juvenile

This swan sized waterbird is the commonest pelican in the Middle East, though it rarely occurs in Arabia, where the Pink-backed Pelican (*Pelecanus rufescens*) is the breeding bird on the Red Sea coast. White plumage, often with an orange tinge, with black flight feathers and yellow-orange throat sac. Juvenile birds are grey-brown above on back and wings and below have dark underwings with a broad, white central panel. Flocks are often seen gliding high in the sky or soaring in warm-air thermals, especially when on migration. During this time, large flocks, sometimes of several thousand, pass through Israel, where some remain in winter.

Dalmatian Pelican *Pelecanus crispus* 170cm

Richard Porter

One of the world's threatened birds, and very rare in Israel. Similar to White Pelican, but has a grey tinge to its plumage and the throat sac in spring is reddish. Also, when seen well, shows short curly tuft of feathers on head. Legs at all ages are grey (pinkish on White Pelican). When soaring or gliding overhead, it shows greyish flight feathers (black on White Pelican) and has a translucent line down centre of underwing. Breeds in small, scattered colonies in Turkey, some dispersing in winter, when individuals occasionally reach Israel.

Little Bittern *Ixobrychus minutus* 36cm

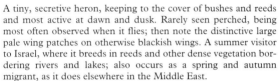

A tiny, secretive heron, keeping to the cover of bushes and reeds and most active at dawn and dusk. Rarely seen perched, being most often observed when it flies; then note the distinctive large pale wing patches on otherwise blackish wings. A summer visitor to Israel, where it breeds in reeds and other dense vegetation bordering rivers and lakes; also occurs as a spring and autumn migrant, as it does elsewhere in the Middle East.

Night Heron *Nycticorax nycticorax* 60cm

A plump heron, much smaller than Grey Heron. Adults are easily told by their grey plumage with black crown and back, although in flight look largely grey. Young birds are brown, heavily spotted white. As the name implies, often seen at dusk, when birds on their breeding grounds utter a deep, frog-like call in flight. Occurs on well-vegetated wetlands and breeds in colonies, often alongside other herons, egrets and even cormorants. Mainly a summer visitor to Israel, where it breeds mostly in the north, especially the Hula. Also breeds on a few lakes in Turkey and widespread in the region on migration.

Cattle Egret *Bubulcus ibis* 50cm

A small, stocky, white heron which is usually seen in flocks in crop fields or grassy meadows, where it frequently associates with cattle. Unlike the other herons and egrets, it is most often seen away from water. In the breeding season, the crown, back and breast feathers take on a strong orange wash and the bill and legs turn red. In all plumages, told from Little Egret by its smaller size, pale bill, and 'jowl' extending below the bill. Patchily distributed throughout the Middle East but increasing in range, and has been a resident breeder in Israel since the 1950s.

Striated Heron *Butorides striatus* 43cm

Richard Porter

A small, dark, coastal heron. The adult is told by its black crown, bluish-grey upperparts and paler greyish neck and underparts. At close range, note a rather marked facial expression. Immature brownish, with streaked underparts and small white tips to some wing feathers; differs from young Night Heron in smaller size, dark crown and lack of prominent white spotting on upperparts. Fairly regular in the Gulf of Eilat, but its main range in the Middle East is the Red Sea and Arabian Gulf.

20

Western Reef Heron *Egretta gularis* 60cm

Slightly larger and less dainty than the Little Egret, and occurs in two main types: white and dark. The white form is very similar to Little Egret, but has a stouter yellowish (not black) bill and greenish-brown legs (black with yellow feet on Little Egret). The dark morph is easily told by its slate-grey plumage with white chin. Can be very active when feeding, making sudden dashes for prey along the tideline or in rock pools. Resident on the coasts of Red Sea, Arabian Sea and Arabian Gulf, where it nests in mangroves and on rocky shores or islands; birds regularly wander to the Gulf of Eilat. Unlike the Little Egret, it is rarely found inland.

Little Egret *Egretta garzetta* 56cm

Slim, elegant white egret about half the size of a Grey Heron. Larger and longer-necked than Cattle Egret and, unlike that species, always found by water. Further told from it and other white heron types by its black bill and black legs with yellow feet, which protrude beyond tail in flight. Occurs in freshwater habitats (the similar Western Reef Heron frequents only coastal shores and marshes) throughout the Middle East in winter and on migration. Good numbers breed in northern Israel, colonially with other herons, in trees.

Great White Egret *Egretta alba* 100cm

The largest of the white herons, resembling a large and long-necked version of the Little Egret, but with a yellow bill and blackish-green legs (no yellow toes). At the onset of the breeding season, the bill becomes dark and often there is a reddish or yellowish flush to the legs. A frequent migrant and winter visitor to Israel, occurring in wetland areas, especially fishponds. It occurs on passage throughout the Middle East with some wintering, but breeding only in central Turkey where it nests colonially in reed beds.

Grey Heron *Ardea cinerea* 90cm

One of the most widespread members of the heron family in the Middle East. Large and grey in colour, as its name implies, but with whitish neck and underparts and black plumes behind the eye. In flight looks very large, with broad, bowed wings, long neck drawn back to body and legs trailing behind. The slightly smaller Purple Heron (*Ardea purpurea*) is darker, with a slimmer, longer, more angular neck and darker purplish or (in young birds) deep buff plumage. Breeds in colonies in trees, but otherwise found on wetland margins. In the Middle East breeds only in Turkey, but on migration and in winter found on most coasts and inland waters throughout the region, including Israel.

Black Stork *Ciconia nigra* 95cm

Similar in size to the White Stork, but instantly told by its black upperparts and black neck (with rest of underparts white), whereas White Stork is white with black flight feathers. Storks fly with neck extended in front and feet projecting behind; by contrast, herons in flight have the neck withdrawn into the body. Forms flocks on migration, circling in the warm-air currents, often with birds of prey. A summer visitor, breeding in woodlands in Turkey. The main migration route between its Eurasian breeding grounds and its wintering area in Africa is through Israel, where a few also winter.

White Stork *Ciconia ciconia* 102cm

A pair of White Storks nesting on a roof or other building is a characteristic sight in Turkey, Iran and most of the Levant, but a far less common one in Israel. An unmistakable species, tall, with a large wingspan, white plumage, black wings and reddish legs and bill. On migration occurs in large flocks, sometimes of many thousands, which soar effortlessly in the warm-air thermals. The main migration routes are through Israel, Lebanon and Turkey, and especially good places to view this spectacle in spring and autumn are Eilat and, in Turkey, the Bosphorus. Winters mostly in Africa, but some remain in Israel.

Glossy Ibis *Plegadis falcinellus* 60cm

A blackish waterbird with long decurved bill. In breeding plumage dark chestnut-brown, glossed with purple and green; outside breeding season dull blackish-brown, with fine white streaks when seen close. Gregarious. Feeds by probing for worms and crustaceans in mud and shallow water in fresh-water marshes. Flies with neck extended in front and feet protruding behind, in line or in V-formation; has fairly rapid wingbeats alternating with long glides. Some winter in Israel and Arabia, where it also occurs on migration; otherwise a summer visitor to its isolated breeding colonies in trees and reedbeds in northern Israel and Turkey.

Alan Williams

Bald Ibis *Geronticus eremita* 75cm

One of the world's most threatened birds, this species survives only in a small semi-wild colony at Biricek in south-east Turkey (plus a few in Morocco) and may also still occur in very small numbers in south-west Arabia. Adults can be told from the Glossy Ibis by their stouter structure, shorter legs, and bare, reddish head with a shaggy mane of feathers. When standing, shows a purple gloss on forewing. Traditionally breeds on cliff ledges with nearby wet grassy areas on which to forage. In Israel, a few have been seen migrating north in spring.

24

Spoonbill *Platalea leucorodia* 85cm

A white, Grey Heron-sized waterbird which is easily identified by its long spoon-shaped bill. In breeding plumage has short crest, yellow patch at base of neck, and black bill with yellowish tip. Juvenile has black wingtips and a pinkish bill. Often occurs in small groups, and feeds by wading in shallow water, sweeping its open bill from side to side to gather insects and small fish. Flies in 'follow-my-leader' style, with neck extended and gliding between bursts of wingbeats. In the Middle East breeds in scattered colonies in Turkey and on the Red Sea coasts, but in Israel is a passage migrant and scarce winter visitor.

Greater Flamingo *Phoenicopterus ruber* 135cm

Unmistakable, with very long neck, long legs and curiously shaped bill. Adult has pale pink plumage with black flight feathers, and pink bill with black tip. Juvenile is pale grey. Feeds by sweeping bill from side to side through water with head upside-down, often submerged. In the Middle East, breeds in dense, isolated colonies on salt lakes in Turkey and Iran. Leaves these in autumn, to spend the winter mainly in coastal areas, especially around Arabia, but in Israel is generally rather scarce.

Greylag Goose *Anser anser* 80cm

Several species of grey geese may occur in the Middle East, but the Greylag is the only one that breeds (in Turkey); it is a rare winter visitor to Israel. The only other goose likely to be encountered is the White-fronted Goose (*Anser albifrons*), which occurs in winter in some strength in areas in the north of the region, with small numbers reaching Israel. All grey geese are very similar, but the Greylag is best told by its large size, large pinkish bill and dull pink legs. It lacks any distinctive features, unlike the Whitefront, which has a white forehead, pink bill, orange legs and black bars on its underparts when adult.

Ruddy Shelduck *Tadorna ferruginea* 65cm

A large duck, easily told by its orange-brown body with paler head and thin black neck-collar and, in flight, by extensive white on wings contrasting with black flight feathers. The female has a paler head and lacks the collar. Legs and bill black. Occurs on lakes and nearby fields, often in large concentrations, especially in winter and on migration. Breeding grounds are mostly in Turkey and Iran, but in winter many birds migrate south, reaching Israel as a rare migrant.

Wigeon *Anas penelope* 48cm

One of the most widespread ducks in the Middle East in winter. The male is easily identified by its chestnut head with prominent yellow forehead and crown, and in flight by the white patch on the forewing. The female is less easy to distinguish from other female ducks, but note the rusty tones, especially on the sides, dark shading around the eye and short grey bill. Wigeons feed by upending in shallow water, but flocks can also frequently be seen grazing on grassy meadows. A winter visitor to most parts of the region, including Israel.

Pintail *Anas acuta* 60cm (plus 10cm tail on male)

The male Pintail is a striking bird with its long tail, long neck and deep brown head, with white breast and a white line running up behind the eye. The drab female lacks the long tail of the male; it is best told by its long neck, grey bill, and plumage similar to a female Mallard (*Anas platyrhynchos*; not illustrated, but a characteristic duck of Europe). Often occurs in large flocks in shallow wetlands, where it upends in its search for food. A winter visitor to most parts of the Middle East, including Israel.

Garganey *Anas querquedula* 38cm

One of the smallest ducks occurring in Israel. The male in breeding plumage is readily identified by its chestnut head and neck with long, broad, white stripe over the eye, extending down onto side of neck. In flight, shows blue-grey forewing. The brown female can be told from similar female Teal (*Anas crecca*) by the whitish patch at base of bill, the dark bar across the cheek and the lack of a white stripe on side of tail. Occurs mostly as a passage migrant throughout Israel and the Middle East, frequenting lakes and marshes; breeds in Turkey.

Shoveler *Anas clypeata* 50cm

The large spatulate bill readily distinguishes the Shoveler from any other duck. In addition, the male can be told by its dark green head, white breast, chestnut underparts and, in flight, blue forewings. Females are brownish (and thus similar to other female ducks), but separated by their huge bill and bluish forewing. A winter visitor and passage migrant to Israel and elsewhere in the Middle East, occurring on marshes, lakes and sewage-treatment pools.

Marbled Teal *Marmaronetta angustirostris* 41cm

A rare, shy duck which is one of the world's threatened birds. Greyish-brown plumage dappled with pale spots and bars, and dark eye patch. Male has a short crest, which is raised during courtship displays. In flight, shows rather long neck and wings. Usually seen in pairs or small groups, often concealed in cover of well-vegetated lakes. A small breeding population resides in the Hula Valley, and in winter birds arrive in other parts of northern Israel from their breeding grounds to the north, notably Turkey.

Red-crested Pochard *Netta rufina* 56cm

A fairly large diving duck, the male of which is easily told by its striking, steep-fronted, orange-brown head, black breast and under-tail-coverts, white body sides and conspicuous red bill. The female (and male in eclipse plumage) is brown, with dark crown and off-white cheeks. Dives for aquatic plants and small animal life, but more frequently upends when feeding. Occurs in flocks on lakes bordered with reeds and other vegetation, marshes and rivers, seldom on the sea. A partial migrant in the Middle East, breeding in Turkey and wintering south to Iraq, with stragglers reaching Israel.

(Above) male; (below) female

Ferruginous Duck *Aythya nyroca* 41cm

A rather uncommon, chestnut diving duck with white undertail-coverts and, in the male, a white eye. Females are browner and duller, with dark eyes; can resemble female Tufted Duck (*Aythya fuligula*), but Ferruginous is smaller, with peaked crown, sloping forehead and long bill. In flight, conspicuous broad white wing-stripe, which extends to wingtip. Found on vegetated lakes, marshes and rivers. Nests occasionally in Israel, but mainly a winter visitor; on passage can be found throughout the Middle East, but always in small numbers.

White-headed Duck *Oxyura leucocephala* 46cm

A small duck with a short neck and long stiff tail, which is often held cocked. The male, with its broad, bright blue bill, white head with black crown and chestnut body, is very easy to identify. The female is duller than the male, with a smaller, greyish bill and a dark bar across the off-white face. Patters at speed across water surface prior to take-off. A rare winter visitor to Israel, breeding in Turkey and Iran on lakes with dense vegetation.

Honey Buzzard *Pernis apivorus* 57cm

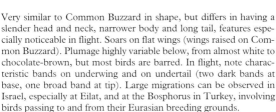

Very similar to Common Buzzard in shape, but differs in having a slender head and neck, narrower body and long tail, features especially noticeable in flight. Soars on flat wings (wings raised on Common Buzzard). Plumage highly variable below, from almost white to chocolate-brown, but most birds are barred. In flight, note characteristic bands on underwing and on undertail (two dark bands at base, one broad band at tip). Large migrations can be observed in Israel, especially at Eilat, and at the Bosphorus in Turkey, involving birds passing to and from their Eurasian breeding grounds.

Black Kite *Milvus migrans* 58cm

A fairly large, dark bird of prey with long wings and a shallow fork in the tail, much shallower than that of the Red Kite (*Milvus milvus*) which is a rare migrant in the Middle East. Plumage dark brown, with paler head and faint brownish bar on upperwing. Agile in flight, with tail frequently twisting and turning; soars with wings held horizontal or slightly bowed. Feeds largely on carrion and offal, and large numbers can be seen around rubbish dumps. In Israel, large migrations can be seen in the spring – especially at Eilat – when birds  pass from their African wintering grounds to breeding areas in Europe and Asia; in addition, some winter and a few pairs breed.

Lammergeier *Gypaetus barbatus* 110cm

A huge vulture, seen singly or in pairs in remote areas. Its long, rather narrow wings and long wedge-shaped tail give a characteristic silhouette. Adults are blackish above, with dull orange underbody and head; black mask through eye, extending into a 'beard' below the bill. Immatures are much duller, with blackish head and greyish underparts. Feeds on carrion, but will also take small mammals. Drops bones from height to smash them and then feed on marrow. A vulture of the mountains, its population appears to be in decline in its Middle East breeding range from Turkey to southern Arabia. A very rare resident in Israel.

Egyptian Vulture *Neophron percnopterus* 60cm

A small vulture, and the only one in the Middle East with a black and white plumage. Adult has white body and tail, black flight feathers, and characteristic thin yellowish bill and yellow face. Young birds are brown overall, but have the same broad wings and blunt wedge-shaped tail as the adult; they take about five years to acquire adult plumage. Often seen in the company of Black Kites at rubbish tips. Breeds throughout much of the Middle East, mainly in mountains, where it nests on rocky ledges. Israel has a small breeding population, but many pass through the country on spring and autumn migrations.

Griffon Vulture *Gyps fulvus* 100cm

One of the largest birds of prey in the Middle East, with long broad wings which bulge at rear edge, and short tail. Told from much rarer Black Vulture (*Aegypius monachus*) by sandy body and under-wing-coverts contrasting with black flight feathers. Also soars with wings raised in a shallow V (flat on Black Vulture). A colonial breeder in mountains, but ranges over open countryside and deserts in search of dead animals on which it feeds. Fairly widespread throughout the Middle East, but uncommon in Israel.

Short-toed Eagle *Circaetus gallicus* 65cm

A large, pale eagle that specializes in catching snakes, hence its other name, Snake-eagle. Typified by broad head, long broad wings, and long tail which has about four prominent bands. The upperparts are brownish, but below it is white – frequently barred brown – with dark wingtips and often a dark head and upper breast. Never shows a dark carpal patch as does Osprey and light form of Honey Buzzard, which are also whitish below. Soars in warm-air thermals and frequently hovers. Summer visitor to hills and lightly wooded plains of Israel and nearby Middle East countries; commoner on migration in spring and autumn.

Marsh Harrier *Circus aeruginosus* 52cm

Harriers are medium-sized birds of prey with long wings and tail which hunt by quartering slowly over the ground or marshland, often making long wavering glides on raised wings. The male Marsh Harrier has a dark reddish-brown body and forewing; the rest of the wings are grey, with black tips. The female is dark brown, with yellowish crown, throat and leading edge of wings. Frequents reedbeds and marshes, but will roam over open countryside during migration. A passage migrant and winter visitor to Israel and the Middle East, where it breeds mostly in Turkey and Iraq.

Pallid Harrier *Circus macrourus* 44cm

Mike McKavett; Windrush Photos

The male is light grey above and white below, with a narrow black wedge on wingtips; told from Montagu's Harrier (*Circus pygargus*) by much cleaner, paler plumage, with black restricted to wingtips. Female is brown, with streaked underparts and a white band at base of uppertail. When seen close, female and juvenile have a pale collar behind dark facial border, a feature that helps separation from corresponding plumages of Montagu's. Juvenile is also unstreaked orange-yellow below. Light flight, low over ground, with glides on wings held in shallow V. Usually seen over fields and marshes. A migrant through Israel and the Middle East, mostly in small numbers.

Levant Sparrowhawk *Accipiter brevipes* 35cm

This summer migrant to the region is difficult to observe except at migration 'hot spots' such as the Bosphorus and Eilat, where many thousands can pass in a few days in spring and autumn. A typical sparrowhawk in shape, but with more pointed wings, giving a falcon-like appearance when gliding. The male is easily told by its almost white underparts and black wingtips. The female is less easy to distinguish from female Eurasian Sparrowhawk (*Accipiter nisus*), but note dark wingtips and dark line down centre of throat. Unlike latter species, it occurs in flocks on migration, which can be observed well in Israel in both spring and autumn.

Common Buzzard *Buteo buteo* 55cm

One of the commonest and most widespread birds of prey to occur in the region at times of migration. A chunky raptor with broad wings and shortish tail which often occurs in flocks outside the breeding season. Soars with raised wings with fully spread tail. Variable in plumage, but two commonest types are dark red-brown or mottled brownish on body and underwing-coverts. In the Middle East breeds only in Turkey, but large migrations there and in Israel in spring and autumn; also winters in Israel.

Long-legged Buzzard *Buteo rufinus* 60cm

Richard Porter

The buzzard of the dry plains, steppes and mountain slopes. Can be difficult to tell from Common Buzzard, but larger and with longer wings which produce a more eagle-like silhouette. Variable in colour, but most birds have a dark belly patch, large dark carpal patch and unbarred orangey tail; some, however, can be blackish-brown with whitish bases to flight feathers and tail. Feeds mostly on rodents and reptiles, and occasionally hovers. Occurs throughout the Middle East, but breeding distribution is patchy and it is uncommon in Israel. Largely resident, although a few migrate from the region into Africa in winter, when it is at its most common in Israel.

Lesser Spotted Eagle *Aquila pomarina* 60cm

Dick Forsman

The commonest eagle on migration in Israel and the Middle East. Very difficult to separate from the other dark brown eagles occurring in the region – Greater Spotted and Steppe Eagles – and identification should be attempted only by experienced observers. Lesser Spotted Eagles can best be seen passing overhead on migration at Eilat and along the edge of the Dead Sea, when many thousands may be recorded in a single day in April or September/October. These are birds moving between their breeding woodlands in Europe and Asia and their wintering grounds in Africa.

Greater Spotted Eagle *Aquila clanga* 67cm

One of the world's threatened eagles for which the Middle East has a special responsibility, as many migrate through or winter in the region. A large bird of prey with uniformly broad wings which are held flat or slightly drooping when gliding and soaring. Adults are entirely blackish-brown; juvenile birds are even darker and have two or three rows of white spots on the upperwing. Differs from Lesser Spotted Eagle in having underwing-coverts darker than flight feathers. Occurs in Israel and throughout the Middle East on migration, but always in small numbers; quite common in winter in Israel, usually at wetlands but elsewhere in the region also at garbage dumps.

Steppe Eagle *Aquila nipalensis* 70cm

One of the largest eagles to be found in the Middle East, but only in the winter or on migration from its breeding grounds in Asia. Much larger than the Greater Spotted Eagle, and with larger bill, longer wings and more protruding head and neck in flight. Adult's plumage is dark brown, with barring on flight feathers and tail. Juvenile easily told from all other birds of prey by broad white band through middle of underwing. Occurs on migration throughout the Middle East (except western Turkey), but largest concentrations are best observed in Israel and north-east Turkey; less common in winter.

Imperial Eagle *Aquila heliaca* 78cm

Richard Porter

One of the world's threatened bird-of-prey species. The Middle East has a particular responsibility for Imperial Eagle because of the numbers that breed in Turkey or occur on migration, especially in Israel or in winter, when it is widespread in the region but in very small numbers. A large, dark brown eagle with long wings and large bill; the crown and hindneck are yellowish, and it has two white 'braces' on the back. Young birds are yellow-brown, streaked darker, and have a pale patch on the primaries below. Soars on flat wings, unlike the similar Golden Eagle (*Aquila chrysaetos*), which soars with wings raised in a V. Nests in tree. Often feeds at rubbish dumps in winter.

Bonelli's Eagle *Hieraaetus fasciatus* 60cm

A medium-sized eagle which is usually seen in pairs or singly in desolate mountain areas. Adults have white underbody and forewing contrasting with otherwise blackish underwing. Above, note white patch on back, though this can be variable in size. Juveniles are buffish below, with usually a narrow dark band through the centre of the wing. Soars and glides with wings held flat, when rather long tail is noticeable. Tends not to wander far from its breeding area; thus very much a resident eagle. Occurs throughout Israel, and has a scattered distribution elsewhere in the Middle East.

Osprey *Pandion haliaetus* 55cm

David Tipling; Windrush Photos

A fish-eating raptor, seen mostly at lakes or in coastal waters. Dives – feet-first – for its prey, often after a brief, rather clumsy hover. Easily told by its dark upperparts and white underparts, with a dark patch at the bend of the wing, and white head with a dark eye-stripe. In Israel and the Middle East occurs, mostly singly, on migration in spring and autumn, but breeds only around the coasts of Arabia on beaches or offshore islands.

Lesser Kestrel *Falco naumanni* 65cm

Richard Porter

The population of this small bird of prey is declining seriously, and it is now listed among the world's threatened birds. Closely resembles Common Kestrel (*Falco tinnunculus*), and the female and immature birds are virtually indistinguishable from that species, although they are slimmer in build and have slightly longer wings and white (not black) claws! The male is more easily told by its blue-grey head (with no black moustache), blue-grey on upper-wing-coverts and unspotted chestnut back. In the Middle East, this is a summer visitor to Israel, Turkey and Jordan, where it breeds colonially in buildings, ruins and holes in cliffs; widespread on migration.

Red-footed Falcon *Falco vespertinus* 30cm

Male

Female

The adult male is slate-grey above and below, with red legs and rusty-red undertail-coverts; it is similar to the Sooty Falcon, but note the reddish undertail-coverts of Red-footed Falcon. The female differs markedly, having orange-buff underparts and underwing-coverts and a dark mask through the eye. On migration usually in flocks, and will often hover when hunting prey. Also takes insects in flight by grabbing them with out-thrust talons. A passage migrant through Israel and countries bordering the Mediterranean, commoner in autumn than in spring.

Hobby *Falco subbuteo* 34cm

Richard Porter

A small falcon similar to the kestrels, but with more scythe-like wings and shorter tail. Upperparts slate-grey without contrast, while underparts are heavily streaked dark, with red thighs, and has black moustache contrasting with white cheeks. Flight fast and agile, especially when hunting birds; catches insects in flight by snatching them with its talons and transferring them to its bill to eat. This migratory falcon is a summer visitor to Israel, where it nests, usually in the old nest of a Hooded Crow, in open woodland and trees in cultivated areas. It also occurs widely in the Middle East on migration.

Sooty Falcon *Falco concolor* 35cm

Richard Porter

This slate-grey falcon arrives on its breeding grounds in the late spring and raises its young in the autumn, thus enabling them to be fed on small birds that are migrating south. It is smaller than a Peregrine Falcon (*Falco peregrinus*), with more slender build, long wings and fairly long tail. The slate-grey plumage is relieved by a yellow base to the bill and orange legs. Hunts mainly at dusk. An uncommon summer visitor to Israel, where it nests from the Dead Sea southwards; elsewhere, occurs in Jordan and Arabia in remote coastal areas and around desert cliffs.

Barbary Falcon *Falco pelegrinoides* 42cm

Dick Forsman

The 'Peregrine Falcon of the desert regions', and some consider it to be just a subspecies of the Peregrine (*Falco peregrinus*). A powerful falcon which stoops at speed on prey, taken mostly in flight. Note the bluish-grey upperparts, buffish underparts narrowly barred on breast and belly, and heavy, dark moustaches; across the back of the neck it is rusty or buffish (unlike Peregrine). Inhabits semi-deserts and arid mountains, also coastal cliffs. Breeds in the southern part of the Middle East, including Israel, Jordan and parts of Arabia.

Chukar *Alectoris chukar* 33cm

A boldly patterned gamebird of stony or rocky slopes, semi-deserts and agricultural fringes. Easily told by its black and white head, white throat bordered by a black necklace, grey breast and vertically striped black and chestnut flanks. Young birds are smaller, greyish, and lack the distinct pattern of the adults. Usually seen in small flocks, and can run swiftly over broken ground. When flushed, flies with fast, whirring wingbeats interspersed with glides. A familiar gamebird in Israel and the Near East, but absent throughout most of Arabia.

Sand Partridge *Ammoperdix heyi* 24cm

(Above) male; (below) female

The partridge of the rocky deserts, with which its colour blends so well. Notably smaller than the Chukar and generally sandy in coloration, the male with bold, sweeping bars of black, white and chestnut on the flanks. Closer views show that the male has a soft blue-grey head and a white patch behind the eye. The female is a dull sandy-grey. Often in small groups, can run fast and most active in the early morning, when its far-carrying 'whipping' song, delivered from a prominent lookout, indicates its presence. Resident in Israel and many areas of Arabia in desolate, rocky and stony country, usually near water; does not occur in sandy deserts.

42

Quail *Coturnix coturnix* 18cm

One of the smallest gamebirds in the region. Rarely seen on the ground, and most usually encountered when it is calling on its breeding grounds or is accidentally flushed from grassland during spring or autumn migration. In flight, it looks small with narrow wings and a striped back; its flight is fast with shallow wingbeats, low over the vegetation. Its song is a characteristic, regularly repeated 'whipping' whistle, *pit, pit-it*, with the accent on the first syllable. A common migrant through Israel and the Middle East, with a few wintering; a rare breeder in northern Israel.

Spotted Crake *Porzana porzana* 23cm

Small crakes can be quite hard to separate unless seen well, which is often difficult as they can be very secretive. The Spotted Crake is best told from the Little (*Porzana parva*) and Baillon's by a combination of its white-spotted plumage, buff under-tail-coverts (can be quite easy to see when bird walking with tail raised), and yellow bill with red base. A spring and autumn migrant in Israel, where it can occur in any wetland areas with reeds and other vegetation; also occurs widely on passage throughout the Middle East.

Baillon's Crake *Porzana pusilla* 18cm

A small crake, little larger than a sparrow. Secretive in its wetland habitat, but on migration can sometimes occur in 'strange' areas such as palm groves, when it is not shy and is easy to observe. It is similar to the Little Crake (*Porzana parva*), which also occurs in the region. The males of both have bluish-grey head and underparts and white spots on the back and bars on the flanks, but the Baillon's has a wholly green bill (red base on Little Crake) and pinkish legs (green on Little). Occurs on migration in Israel and throughout the Middle East, although rarely seen because of its usually skulking habits.

Purple Gallinule *Porphyrio porphyrio* 45cm

A large waterbird, the size of a chicken, that is easily told by its bluish-green plumage and, usually, greyish head. The bill is bright red and the legs pinkish-red. Feeds on wetland vegetation, which it tugs at with its strong legs and strips with its powerful bill. There is some suggestion that, with the shrinking of the marshlands of Iraq (a major breeding area), birds are spreading elsewhere. An occasional visitor to Israel, probably from breeding areas in southern Turkey, Iraq and the Nile Valley, where it occurs in swamps with extensive reedbeds.

44

Coot *Fulica atra* 38cm

An all-black waterbird with white bill and white shield on fore-head. Can be confused only with the Moorhen (*Gallinula chloropus*), but that species is smaller, with a red bill and frontal shield, a white line along the side and white undertail-coverts. Young Coots lack the white frontal shield and have greyish-white underparts. Coots often gather in large concentrations in the winter. Occurs on large areas of open fresh water, where it breeds in vegetation in shallow water. In Israel, it is a common migrant and winter visitor, with a few nesting in the north.

Common Crane *Grus grus* 115cm

David Tipling; Windrush Photos

A large bird with a long neck, indeed the tallest-standing bird occurring in the Middle East. The plumage is grey, with a red crown patch and a black head with white stripe down side of upper neck; a large tuft of blackish plumes hangs over the tail. Differs from Demoiselle Crane (*Anthropoides virgo*) in larger size and grey, not black, breast. In flight, the extended neck and legs appear to droop below the level of the body. Has powerful wingbeats with long glides, and flocks are often in V-formation, especially on migration. Breeds in scattered colonies in Turkey, but occurs throughout the region on migration, especially in Israel, where it also winters.

Houbara Bustard *Chlamydotis undulata* 60cm

The largest gamebird traditionally hunted in Arabia, and numbers have declined markedly in recent decades. Very well adapted to its desert environment, where its cryptic coloration makes it difficult to detect on the ground. When disturbed, it usually walks away or crouches very low to the ground. Long-tailed and long-necked, with sandy-buff upperparts with dark vermiculations and a black stripe down side of neck. In flight, shows black flight feathers with bright white patch near wingtip. A scarce resident in Israel, mainly in the Judean and Negev Deserts; elsewhere in the Middle East, breeds patchily in northern and eastern Arabia, numbers increasing in winter with the arrival of migrants from Central Asia.

Painted Snipe *Rostratula benghalensis* 25cm

David Tipling; Windrush Photos

This species is unusual in that the female is more brightly coloured than the male, with chestnut breast and neck, which are separated from brownish-olive upperparts by a conspicuous sweep of white from the breast to the back; note also the white eye-ring. In the male, the chestnut is replaced by grey-buff and the upperparts are barred brownish. A bird of vegetated swamps and reedbeds, where it nests, but will venture out into the open. Resident in the Nile Delta, and a vagrant to Israel and Arabia.

Black-winged Stilt *Himantopus himantopus* 38cm

A tall-standing, elegant, black and white wader with a fine black bill and extremely long, thin, pink legs. Occurs on shallow freshwater or brackish marshes and lagoons, and has very delicate movements. Very noisy when on eggs or with young. Breeds in scattered colonies in Israel and throughout the Middle East, but less commonly in Arabia; widespread on passage and in winter.

Avocet *Recurvirostra avosetta* 43cm

A truly elegant wader, easily told by its white and black plumage and long, upcurved bill, which it sweeps through shallow water in search of prey: invertebrates on or near the surface. When agitated on its breeding grounds, its call is a persistent, ringing *pleet*, uttered as it flies round overhead. Nests colonially, usually in saline areas. A casual breeder in Israel and seen mostly on spring and autumn migration; occurs throughout the Middle East, especially on coasts, on migration and in winter, but only breeds in numbers in Turkey.

47

Stone-curlew *Burhinus oedicnemus* 42cm

A large, brownish, dryland wader with short bill and staring yellow eye. Very similar Spotted Thick-knee (*Burhinus capensis*) of southern Arabia has upperparts spotted with black and lacks black and white bars on closed and open wing. Senegal Thick-knee (*Burhinus senegalensis*), which breeds in Egypt, even on rooftops, lacks the white band on wing and has plain rufous or greyish uppertail. Inhabits open plains and semi-deserts. A fairly common breeding bird in Israel, where mostly resident, it also breeds in neighbouring east Mediterranean countries; on migration and in winter, found in small numbers throughout the Middle East.

Cream-coloured Courser *Cursorius cursor* 20cm

Well adapted to life in the desert, and appropriately camouflaged in its sandy-buff plumage. Note the head pattern and, in flight, black wingtips above and all-dark underwings. Runs away quickly, and then abruptly stops to stand upright. Occurs in sandy or stony semi-deserts, or on cultivation in winter. A locally common breeding summer visitor to Israel, where it also occurs in small numbers in winter; breeds thinly throughout much of the Middle East, except Turkey, and more widespread on migration and in winter.

Collared Pratincole *Glareola pratincola* 25cm

A fork-tailed wader with short bill and legs, resembling a tern in flight. The Collared Pratincole has chestnut-orange underwings and white trailing edge of wing, whereas the very similar Black-winged Pratincole (*Glareola nordmanni*) has black underwing and no white trailing edge; both have a white rump. A bird of dry plains and baked mud-flats, and often seen in flocks chasing flying insects. A summer visitor to scattered colonies in north Israel and throughout much of the western part of the Middle East; otherwise a fairly widespread migrant.

Little Ringed Plover *Charadrius dubius* 15cm

Very similar to the Ringed Plover (*Charadrius hiaticula*) in having a complete black breast-band on otherwise white underparts, a black eye-mask and a white collar around back of neck. Little Ringed can be easily separated by its yellow eye-ring and absence of white wingbar in flight. Mainly a summer visitor to Israel, where it breeds in the north on the margins of freshwater rivers and lakes; elsewhere in the Middle East, it occurs on migration, with small numbers in winter, and breeds widely in Turkey but at scattered sites elsewhere.

49

Kentish Plover *Charadrius alexandrinus* 16cm

A small sandy and white wader, the male of which has neat black markings on its head and neck, and a ginger wash to the crown. One of the characteristic waders of the region's shorelines. It is smaller than the sand plovers, and lacks the complete black breast-band of the Ringed (*Charadrius hiaticula*) and Little Ringed Plovers. Occurs on dry mudflats and coastal beaches. A resident or partial migrant which is widespread throughout the Middle East, but absent in central Arabia; in Israel it is a scarce breeder, mainly in the north.

Greater Sand Plover *Charadrius leschenaultii* 23cm

Larger than Kentish Plover and smaller than Grey Plover, this shorebird is most easily told in summer plumage, when it shows a chestnut breast-band and black mark through the eye. Otherwise rather nondescript, like a large version of female Kentish Plover, but never shows a white neck-ring. Similar to, but slightly larger than, the Lesser Sand Plover (*Charadrius mongolus*), which has occurred only twice in Israel. A summer visitor to isolated breeding colonies in Turkey, Jordan and Syria; elsewhere, including Israel, a passage migrant and winter visitor.

50

Caspian Plover *Charadrius asiaticus* 19cm

This elegant plover bears some resemblance to the Greater Sand Plover, but has longer wings and legs, and smaller head with a finer bill. The non-breeding plumage is similar to that of the sand plovers, but the white stripe above the eye is broader and the breast-band more distinct. In summer plumage the male is handsome, with a deep rufous breast-band bordered black below. In all plumages the underwing is dusky, providing further separation from the sand plovers. An uncommon migrant in Israel and elsewhere in the Middle East, occurring in fields and grassy areas bordering wetlands.

Grey Plover *Pluvialis squatarola* 28cm

Alan Williams

A large coastal wader with short black bill. In summer plumage (in which many spring migrants will appear), it is easily told by its grey-spangled upperparts and black underparts; in winter, its underparts become white. The golden plovers – European Golden and Pacific Golden (*Pluvialis apricaria* and *P. fulva*) – are much rarer in the Middle East and are always told by their golden-brown upperparts; they also lack the black patch at the base of the underwing shown by the Grey Plover in flight. A passage migrant and winter visitor to the coasts of Israel and the Middle East; rarely seen inland.

51

Spur-winged Plover *Hoplopterus spinosus* 26cm

A long-legged, short-billed upright plover with black upper head, conspicuous white neck and upper breast, and black line joining bill to black lower breast, belly and flanks. In flight, sandy-brown coverts are separated from black flight feathers by broad white band. Wing pattern is thus similar to that of White-tailed and Red-wattled Plovers (*Chettusia leucura* and *Hoplopterus indicus*), but former lacks black on underparts and has an all-white tail, while latter has white belly, red bill and red skin on face; both also have yellow legs. A resident breeder in Israel and locally in the Middle East, where it also occurs on migration. In recent decades has been extending its breeding range in the region.

Sociable Plover *Chettusia gregaria* 28cm

Richard Porter

One of the world's threatened waders that occurs in the Middle East. About the size of a Lapwing (*Vanellus vanellus*), but with a more upright stance, grey-brown upperparts, black crown, long white stripe over eye and chestnut belly patch; last feature is lost in much plainer winter plumage. In flight, shows a wing pattern very similar to Spur-winged Plover's. Often occurs in small groups or even singly among flocks of Lapwing or European Golden Plover (*Pluvialis apricaria*). A scarce passage migrant and winter visitor from its Asian breeding grounds to Israel and the Middle East, where it is found in semi-deserts, as well as cultivated and ploughed fields.

Little Stint *Calidris minuta* 13cm

Together with Temminck's Stint (*Calidris temminckii*), this is the smallest wader to be found in the Middle East. It has a short black bill and black legs, whereas Temminck's has yellowish legs. In summer plumage, upperparts are spangled chestnut and black, with a pale V-marking on the back; in non-breeding season, it is greyish above and white below. Often seen in flocks of many hundreds. Occurs on migration and in winter in Israel and throughout the Middle East, but particularly on the coastal mudflats; Temminck's Stint is more frequently found on freshwater marshes.

Curlew Sandpiper *Calidris ferruginea* 19cm

A small shorebird, slightly larger than Dunlin (*Calidris alpina*) and with longer legs and longer, more decurved bill; easily told from it in all plumages by white rump visible in flight. In summer, a beautiful brick-red from head to belly, with black streaking on crown and back; in winter, however, pale grey above and white below, thus similar to Dunlin but much cleaner looking. Usually seen in small flocks on coastal mudflats and estuaries, where it wades in shallow water up to its belly. Found mainly on spring and autumn passage in Israel and coastal Arabia, where it also winters.

(Above) summer; (below) winter

53

Broad-billed Sandpiper *Limicola falcinellus* 17cm

A fairly small shoreline wader, slightly smaller than a Dunlin (*Calidris alpina*), from which it is told in all plumages by its longer bill with downward droop at tip and shorter, yellowish-grey (not black) legs. Close views show a double supercilium. In winter it is a basically grey bird, but in summer rather dark brownish with noticeably dark-spotted breast and sides. Often in small flocks with other waders. A rare passage migrant in Israel; elsewhere in the Middle East, can be fairly common on migration and in winter in UAE, Oman and southern Arabia.

Ruff *Philomachus pugnax* 26cm

Highly variable in breeding plumage, when the larger males have colourful ear-tufts and ruffs in various colours: white, black, chestnut or purple. Otherwise a fairly plain wader with greyish-brown upperparts and buff-mottled white underparts. The head is rather small, the bill dark and the legs usually orange. In flight, which is rather lazy, has a faint wingbar and two white ovals at base of tail. Often in flocks. A bird of inland marshes, rarely seen on coastal shores. Does not breed in the Middle East but is found on migration throughout, including Israel.

Common Snipe *Gallinago gallinago* 28cm

A well-camouflaged wader with very long bill. The plumage is a mixture of browns, and the face has a dark eye-stripe and cheek-bar; the flanks are barred. In fast zigzagging flight listen out for the rasping call. Much smaller than the rarer Great Snipe (*Gallinago media*) and larger than the Jack Snipe (*Lymnocryptes minimus*), which is also less common. Rarely seen on the coast, being a bird of freshwater marshes and other inland wetlands. Does not breed in Israel or the Middle East, but is a passage migrant and winter visitor to the whole area.

Bar-tailed Godwit *Limosa lapponica* 38cm

A large shoreline wader with long, slightly upcurved bill. In breeding plumage (shown by many spring migrants) is a deep reddish-brown on head and underparts; this colour is lost in winter, when it becomes streaked brownish-grey. In flight, easily told from otherwise similar Black-tailed Godwit (*Limosa limosa*) by brownish upperwing and white rump, whereas Black-tailed has broad white wingbar and black tail-band. Frequents coastal mudflats and estuaries. Does not breed in the Middle East, but occurs on passage and in winter, although less common in Israel than around the coasts of Arabia.

Whimbrel *Numenius phaeopus* 41cm

A fairly large, brown wader with a long decurved bill. It resembles the Curlew (*Numenius arquata*), but is smaller and darker, has a shorter bill and also has a characteristic dark stripe on the side of its crown. In flight, note the dark wings, white on rump extending up back and, especially, the seven-note whistling call. Often associates with other waders on coastal mudflats and estuaries. Does not breed in the Middle East but occurs on passage throughout, including Israel.

Slender-billed Curlew *Numenius tenuirostris* 40cm

(Above) Slender-billed Curlew; (below) Curlew

Slightly smaller and more delicate than Whimbrel and especially smaller than Curlew (*Numenius arquata*). It is a very neat bird with fine, tapering bill, and white underparts with small black spots on sides; also dark grey legs (darker than blue-grey of Curlew). Occurs most typically on wet grassland. One of the rarest and most endangered waders in the world. Formerly commoner but now a very rare winter visitor to the Middle East, and there is only one record from Israel – in 1917 – but, with the increase in birdwatchers, it could be found again.

Redshank *Tringa totanus* 28cm

A medium-sized wader of the shoreline, told by its red legs and mostly red bill. In flight it is noisy, and its loud, shrill *tue-ew* call often gives away its presence; it also shows a broad white wingbar and white rump. Nests among tussocks on inland wetlands, but otherwise a typical wader of coastal estuaries. In the Middle East, breeds only in Turkey; otherwise a widespread passage migrant and winter visitor throughout, including Israel.

Marsh Sandpiper *Tringa stagnatilis* 23cm

A medium-sized wader, slimmer than a Redshank, with slender neck, long greenish legs and needle-like blackish bill. In flight, it shows all-dark upperwings and square white rump. It is most similar to a Greenshank (*Tringa nebularia*), but that is larger and has a slightly upcurved bill. Rarely found on the coast, occurring mostly on freshwater marshes and the edges of pools. Does not breed in the Middle East, but found in small numbers on migration throughout, including Israel.

Wood Sandpiper *Tringa glareola* 20cm

Told from the other small to medium-sized sandpipers by its brownish upperparts spangled with whitish spots, yellowish legs and straight black bill. In flight, note the dark upperwings and white rump. Similar to the Green Sandpiper (*Tringa ochropus*), but that has much darker upperparts and, in flight, blackish underwings. Often occurs in flocks, and can be very common. Found mostly on the edges of freshwater marshes, rarely on the coast. Widespread on spring and autumn migration throughout the Middle East, including Israel.

Terek Sandpiper *Xenus cinereus* 23cm

Richard Porter

A rather stout wader with long upcurved bill and short yellowish legs. Very active and restless when feeding, often making fast runs with head held low; tail constantly bobbed. Upperparts are pale brownish-grey with black lines on back; plumage is paler in winter. In flight, shows white trailing edge to wing. Occurs on passage throughout the Middle East, but less common in Israel; winters mainly on the coast of Arabia, particularly favouring mudflats and mangrove creeks.

Common Sandpiper *Actitis hypoleucos* 20cm

A fairly small sandpiper with short legs and long tail. Its most characteristic features are the white area separating the brownish breast from the wings, and the almost constant bobbing of its tail. In flight, which is usually low over the water, note the rapid flickering wingbeats alternating with glides on stiffly held wings. Usually seen singly or in very small groups. In the Middle East, breeds in eastern Turkey on mountain rivers; otherwise a passage migrant and winter visitor throughout the region, including Israel.

Red-necked Phalarope *Phalaropus lobatus* 18cm

This small, delicate wader is one of the most easily recognized of the Middle East. Swims and bobs on water, sometimes in very large concentrations, its needle-like bill rapidly pecking for food from the surface. In the breeding plumage, note the rufous-red sides of neck and white throat, while in winter it has a characteristic black crown and black patch through the eye. A maritime species outside the breeding season, but occurs also on inland lakes on migration. A scarce migrant in Israel, but common on passage in the Arabian Gulf and the seas around eastern Arabia.

(Above) summer; (below) winter

Sooty Gull *Larus hemprichii* 43cm

Probably the most characteristic gull of the seas around Arabia, but very rare in Israel. Superficially resembles the White-eyed Gull, but larger, with stouter, two-tone bill, which is pale yellowish with a black tip. Its head and upperparts are sooty-brown. Sooty Gull lacks the white eye-ring of White-eyed Gull, but it does have a short white crescent above the eye, and sometimes below it. A coastal gull found throughout the year in the Red Sea and Arabian Gulf, especially around fishing ports, though surprisingly only four or five records from Israel.

White-eyed Gull *Larus leucophthalmus* 41cm

Also known as the Red Sea Gull, this bird is endemic to the Middle East. Told from the similar Sooty Gull by its slightly smaller size, and, in adult plumage, all-black hood and bib, dark grey upperparts, all-dark bill (dark red with black tip, unlike two-tone bill of Sooty Gull) and conspicuous white eye-ring. In flight, shows a dark underwing, like Sooty Gull. The range is virtually confined to the Red Sea, where it breeds colonially on offshore islands, non-breeding birds frequently wandering to the Gulf of Eilat.

Great Black-headed Gull *Larus ichthyaetus* 59cm

The largest gull that occurs in the Middle East. Easily told in breeding plumage by large size, pale grey back and wings, black hood and orange-yellow bill; in winter, the head is white with dark eye patch. Immatures are more difficult to separate from other similar-looking immature gulls, but the large size, long, sloping forehead, large dark bill and brownish hindneck and sides of neck are helpful. Occurs on coastal flats and occasionally inland lakes. A winter visitor to northern Israel, as well as the seas around Arabia; less frequent elsewhere.

Mediterranean Gull *Larus melanocephalus* 37cm

Richard Porter

Like a small version of the Great Black-headed Gull, but with red bill and all-white wings in adult plumage. In autumn and winter the black hood is lost, and it then has a broad dark eye-streak. Young birds are difficult to distinguish from Black-headed Gull, but they are larger, have a black mark flaring behind the eye, and the bill is stouter and slightly drooping. A coastal species, but breeds on inland lakes. A scarce migrant and winter visitor to Israel and neighbouring east Mediterranean countries; in the Middle East, breeds only in Turkey.

Black-headed Gull *Larus ridibundus* 35cm

Similar to the Mediterranean Gull, but note the slightly smaller size, slimmer, straighter bill, brown (not black) head and black on undersides of wingtips. In winter the brown hood is lost, and it then has just a dark spot behind the eye. Often occurs in flocks and congregates with other gulls, especially around fishing ports or where fish catches are brought in from the sea. In the Middle East breeds in Turkey, but otherwise widespread on migration and in winter on all coasts and many lakes of the region, including Israel.

Lesser Black-backed Gull *Larus fuscus* 52–67cm

Richard Porter

A fairly large gull, easily told in adult plumage by its white body and dark back and wings, with white spots on wingtip. The legs are yellow, and the bill yellow with a red spot. Young birds are dark brownish above, with a white rump and dark tail. Several subspecies of Lesser Black-backed Gull occur in the Middle East, and there is much debate as to their taxonomy and status. The bird depicted here is of the race *heuglini*. It associates with other gulls on beaches and around fishing ports. A winter visitor to all coasts of the Middle East, including Israel.

Yellow-legged Gull *Larus michahellis* 55–67cm

A familiar gull of the Mediterranean, especially in winter. Larger than the Black-headed Gull, with white body, grey upperparts, yellow legs, and yellow bill with red spot at tip. The wingtips are black with white spots. Juvenile birds are similar to young Lesser Black-backed Gulls, but less dark. Like all gulls, is gregarious, especially around fishing ports. Breeds on the northern coast of Israel and in winter birds arrive from their northern breeding grounds, including numbers of the very similar Caspian Gull (*Larus cachinnans*).

Gull-billed Tern *Gelochelidon nilotica* 38cm

Richard Porter

Shows some resemblance to both Sandwich Tern and Common Tern, but upperparts are entirely whitish-grey, with narrow dark trailing edge to outer flight feathers. When seen close, the rather stout, gull-like black bill is characteristic. The black cap is lost in winter, when there is just a black patch behind the eye. Unlike other terns, it can often be found hunting insects over the grassy margins of wetlands. A passage migrant through Israel and the Middle East, with some breeding in the Arabian Gulf and Turkey.

Caspian Tern *Sterna caspia* 53cm

The largest tern, and easily identified by its large, heavy, bright red bill and, in flight, by the black undersurface of its primary feathers. In winter, the otherwise black cap takes on a white forehead and the crown becomes streaked with white. The slightly smaller Swift Tern (*Sterna bergii*), very rare in Israel, has long, slightly drooping, yellowish bill and ashy-grey upperparts. The flight is powerful, and it dives ably for fish from a height of about 10m above the water. This mainly coastal species is a scarce passage migrant through Israel; commoner on migration elsewhere in the Middle East, it also breeds in Turkey, the Red Sea and the Arabian Gulf.

Sandwich Tern *Sterna sandvicensis* 41cm

A medium-sized white tern, and the most widespread tern in coastal areas of the Middle East in autumn, winter and spring. Easily told from all other terns by its black bill with yellow tip. In breeding plumage, has a full black cap with rather shaggy feathers on the nape, but by autumn the forehead is white. Note that the rather similar Lesser Crested Tern (*Sterna bengalensis*) has an orange-yellow bill. The Sandwich Tern does not breed in the Middle East, but is found on migration on most coasts, rarely inland, including in Israel.

64

Common Tern *Sterna hirundo* 36cm

Smaller than Sandwich Tern, with slimmer wings and pale grey upperparts. Like all terns, it has a forked tail. When breeding, the cap is black and the bill red with a black tip; in winter plumage, the forehead becomes white and the bill blackish. Usually in flocks, and often hovers before diving for fish. In the Middle East occurs on inland wetlands in the breeding season, but largely coastal at other times. A summer visitor to breeding colonies in Israel and neighbouring Mediterranean countries as well as Turkey; widespread on migration in the region and often the commonest tern.

Little Tern *Sterna albifrons* 24cm

Along with Saunders's Tern (*Sterna saundersi*), this is the smallest tern to be found in the Middle East. Readily told by its tiny size, short forked tail, black cap and eye-stripe with white forehead, and yellow bill with black tip. Another helpful feature is its fast wing-beats. In Mediterranean areas it is mainly coastal, breeding on sand or shingle beaches, but otherwise found on inland lakes and wide stony rivers, especially in Turkey. A summer visitor to scattered colonies in north Israel and neighbouring east Mediterranean countries; occurs more widely on passage.

Whiskered Tern *Chlidonias hybridus* 25cm

Can easily be confused with Black Tern (*Chlidonias niger*) and White-winged Black Tern in winter plumage, but note that Whiskered has broader wings and heavier bill. In summer plumage quite distinct, with grey underparts which contrast with white stripe on cheeks and white underwings. A spring and autumn passage migrant through Israel but, unlike the Black and White-winged Black Terns, it also winters in small numbers; elsewhere in the Middle East it is also a passage migrant, with small numbers wintering, occurring mainly on inland waters.

White-winged Black Tern *Chlidonias leucopterus* 24cm

In breeding plumage, this is a most striking bird. The black head, body and underwing-coverts contrast with the white tail and, especially, the white upperwing. In autumn and winter it is more soberly plumaged, with white underparts, grey upperparts and a small black crown and ear patch; in this plumage, it is very difficult to separate from the Black Tern (*Chlidonias niger*) and Whiskered Tern. Highly gregarious, and frequents freshwater lakes and slow-flowing rivers. A passage migrant through Israel and most of the Middle East, with breeding colonies in Turkey and Iraq.

Lichtenstein's Sandgrouse *Pterocles lichtensteinii* 25cm

This is one of six species of sandgrouse that breed in the Middle East. Sandgrouse are one of the specialists of the desert, expertly camouflaged and with water-absorbent breast feathers to carry water from drinking holes back to their young. Lichtenstein's gather to drink mainly at dusk, whereas the other sandgrouse assemble at waterholes mainly in the early morning. Note the short, square tail, barred upperparts and head pattern of Lichtenstein's. A bird of dry, rocky semi-deserts with trees, especially acacias. Resident in Eilat area of southern Israel and in scattered localities throughout the Middle East.

Crowned Sandgrouse *Pterocles coronatus* 28cm

One of five species of sandgrouse that breed in Israel; apart from the Spotted Sandgrouse (*Pterocles senegallus*), all are illustrated in this guide. The Crowned and Spotted are similar, but the Crowned has sandy wings with black flight feathers (generally rather pale upperwing on Spotted); also, Crowned has a short tail which is noticeably white-tipped when spread on landing, whereas Spotted has a long pointed tail. The male Crowned has a characteristic black surround to the base of the bill. Both species are birds of semi-deserts and are resident in southern Israel, where they gather in large flocks at drinking pools. They have a patchy distribution in the Middle East.

Black-bellied Sandgrouse *Pterocles orientalis* 34cm

A plump sandgrouse and the largest to occur in the Middle East. In Israel it is the easiest to identify, with its all-black belly contrasting with pale breast and neck, and white under-wings with black wingtips. In flight, note the characteristic bub-bling call. Often occurs singly or in small groups, but flocks of several hun-dred will gather at drink-ing pools. Inhabits dry plains with sparse vege-tation, breeding in cen-tral Israel; elsewhere in the Middle East, it occurs only in Cyprus and Turkey.

(Top) male;
(bottom) female

Pin-tailed Sandgrouse *Pterocles alchata* 37cm

(Above) male; (below) female

Has the longest tail of the Middle East sand-grouse, a feature that distinguishes it from the Crowned and the Spotted Sandgrouse (*Pterocles senegallus*). All three are daytime fliers and show pale or whitish underparts with dark wingtips in flight, which, like that of all sandgrouse, is fast and direct. Pin-tailed also has a clearly demarcated chestnut or buff breast, whereas the other two have uniform greyish underparts. Occurs in stony deserts, often near cultivation and in very large, vocal flocks. Resi-dent in Israel and local-ly in the east Mediter-ranean and northern Saudi Arabia.

Rock Dove *Columba livia* 33cm

The 'pure' wild form of this dove is found typically in rocky upland areas and on coastal cliffs in Israel and elsewhere in the Middle East. The highly variable feral form (the typical town pigeon) can be found almost anywhere associated with human habitation. A medium-sized pigeon in which the pure form is blue-grey with two black bands on the upperwing, a white or grey rump and white underwing. It thus differs from the similar Stock Dove (*Columba oenas*) in its white underwing and rump and long black wingbars (short on Stock Dove). Occurs throughout Israel and the Middle East, nearly always in flocks.

Collared Dove *Streptopelia decaocto* 28cm

A pale grey-buff dove that is one of the commonest to be seen in most parts of the region except in the south, where it is replaced by the very similar African Collared Dove (*Streptopelia roseogrisea*). Easily told by its pale greyish-buff plumage and black (with white border) half-collar. Where it occurs it can often be seen in large flocks, particularly in areas where there is a supply of grain, such as farmsteads. Frequents towns, villages and settlements and near-by agricultural areas. A common resident in Israel with a patchy distribution elsewhere in the Middle East, mostly in the northern part, being absent in southern Arabia.

69

Turtle Dove *Streptopelia turtur* 27cm

The commonest dove to be seen on migration in Israel, often in large numbers. Unfortunately, in many areas it is a popular bird for hunting. The most important features for identification are the rufous upperparts with black feather centres, pale purplish-pink neck and breast, and black and white barred patch on sides of neck. Flight is rapid and agile, and flutters wings and fans tail during take-off and landing. The song is a soft purring, often for long periods. It seeks open country with bushes and scattered trees. A summer visitor to Israel and the Middle East, breeding in Turkey, the east Mediterranean and parts of northern Arabia.

Laughing Dove *Streptopelia senegalensis* 26cm

A small, rather dark dove and the one that is likely to be encountered most often in villages and towns throughout the region. It is smaller and darker than the Turtle Dove, with shorter wings and longer tail. The plumage is a smooth pinkish-brown above, with blue-grey panels in the wing; the dull pinkish underparts have an orange-brown throat speckled with black. Its song is usually of five syllables, *doo, doo, dooh, dooh, do*, with the third and fourth notes longer and higher in tone. Resident throughout Israel and much of the Middle East.

Namaqua Dove *Oena capensis* 29cm (incl. 9cm tail)

The smallest dove in the Middle East, and in flight reminiscent of a small greyish parakeet. Unmistakable: small, with long black tail, and chestnut patch in wing when it flies. The male has a black face

(Top) male; (bottom) female

and upper breast and an orange bill. The flight is very fast and direct. Often in small flocks, and spends much time on the ground. Song is a mournful *hu-hu, hu-hu*. A scarce breeder in Israel, which it has recently colonized from Arabia, where its range is expanding as deserts are converted to agriculture.

Ring-necked Parakeet *Psittacula krameri* 42cm

Richard Porter

A bright green parakeet with long tail and heavy, deeply hooked red bill. The male is told by its black throat and rosy ring around its neck. Often seen in flocks, which are fast-flying and noisy, the bird having a shrill, screaming *kee-ek* call. Inhabits gardens and plantations, where it feeds on fruits and nests in holes in trees. A non-native species in the Middle East, having originally escaped from captivity. There are now a number of colonies in towns and settlements throughout Israel.

Great Spotted Cuckoo *Clamator glandarius* 40cm

Like all cuckoos, this species lays its eggs in the nests of other birds, in this case in the nests of crows and Magpies. A long-tailed cuckoo with prominent crest; dark grey above, with wings spotted white, and white below, with a soft yellowish wash on the throat and breast. Young birds lack the crest and have orange flight feathers, noticeable in flight. Olive groves and open areas with bushes and trees are its favoured habitat. A passage migrant and uncommon breeding summer visitor to Israel and neighbouring countries in the Middle East.

Common Cuckoo *Cuculus canorus* 33cm

The Common Cuckoo lays its eggs in the nests of small songbirds such as buntings and warblers, and leaves the latter with the task of raising its young. Long-tailed and narrow-winged, with grey upperparts and breast; rest of underparts white with narrow grey bars. Females can occur with reddish-brown upperparts – similar to young birds, though these have pale fringes to the feathers. The call, *cuckoo, cuck-oo*, is a characteristic sound in the breeding areas. Occurs in open country with trees and woodland edges. Widespread on migration throughout the Middle East, and breeding in Israel and neighbouring east Mediterranean countries.

European Scops Owl *Otus scops* 19cm

A small, slim owl with ear-tufts that is more often heard than seen, as it is strictly nocturnal. During daylight, it will often roost close to the trunk of a tree. One can then see its grey-brown plumage, finely vermiculated, and with delicate black streaks on a complex pattern of fine bars below. Song is a far-carrying whistle, repeated every few seconds, a characteristic sound of summer nights. A summer visitor to its breeding grounds in Israel and other countries of the east Mediterranean. Two other species of scops owl occur in the Middle East: Striated Scops Owl (*Otus brucei*), rare in Israel, and African Scops Owl (*Otus senegalensis*) of south Arabia.

Alan Williams

Eagle Owl *Bubo bubo* 70cm

Like most owls, rarely seen in the daytime unless discovered at roost or when accidentally flushed. Dawn and dusk are the best times to see it. The largest owl in the region, with long, broad wings, pronounced ear-tufts, orange eyes and brown, streaked plumage. Often the first indication of its presence is its song at night, a far-carrying deep *hoo-hoo*, repeated every few seconds. Occurs in mountains and desert steppes, nesting on rocky ledge or crevice in rocks. An uncommon resident in Israel, and with a patchy distribution throughout the Middle East.

Little Owl *Athene noctua* 22cm

Another small owl but, unlike the European Scops Owl, is often seen in daylight, especially around dawn and dusk. It is rather plump in shape, with a rounded head (lacks ear-tufts), and frequently bobs up and down, especially when agitated. Plumage is brown above, spotted with white, and white below with broad dark brown streaking. Flight is undulating, unlike that of other owls of the region. It frequents open country with trees, stony wastelands and rocky semi-deserts, nesting in holes in tree, rock or building. Widespread resident throughout Israel and the Middle East, though absent from areas of sandy desert.

Hume's Tawny Owl *Strix butleri* 35cm

Paul Doherty

This is the only species of owl that is endemic to the Middle East. Highly nocturnal and therefore likely to be discovered only by its song: a five-note hoot, *whoo, woo-woo, who-who*. It is similar in shape to Tawny Owl (*Strix aluco*), which is a rare breeder in wooded areas of northern Israel, but is smaller and much paler, being sandy-buff with a greyish back; its eyes are orange-yellow (dark in Tawny Owl). A resident in rather isolated rocky deserts and gorges in Israel and several areas of Arabia. Recent surveys have shown that its range is more extensive than previously thought.

European Nightjar *Caprimulgus europaeus* 26cm

Nightjars are night birds and best located and identified by their songs. Three species occur in Israel, of which the European Nightjar (which breeds in Turkey) is the most likely to be encountered during spring and autumn migration. It is the largest and darkest of the nightjars and has a churring song. The smallest, the Nubian Nightjar (*Caprimulgus nubicus*), shows much chestnut in the wing in flight and has a characteristic song, a double-note *quil-quil*, repeated for long periods at night; it breeds in desert areas with scattered vegetation in southern Israel and southern Arabia.

Egyptian Nightjar *Caprimulgus aegyptius* 25cm

Tim Loseby

The palest nightjar to occur in Israel and the Middle East. On the ground, it is sandy-coloured with paler feather edgings and with fine, black streaks on the crown and upperparts. In flight, appears very pale below, especially on the underwing, while dark flight feathers above contrast with the rest of the pale plumage. Unlike the other nightjars in the region, neither sex shows white wing patches. A vagrant to Israel, breeding in the Middle East only in Iraq and probably Jordan; found on migration throughout Arabia.

75

Pallid Swift *Apus pallidus* 16cm

The Pallid Swift and Common Swift (*Apus apus*) are difficult to distinguish. Both are summer visitors to Israel, but the Common Swift breeds in the north and central parts, whereas the Pallid occurs in scattered colonies in the south and east, mainly in cliffs in isolated areas. The Pallid Swift, when seen well, is lighter in colour than the Common Swift, the plumage being brownish with paler flight feathers, and it has a larger pale throat patch. Like Common Swift, often seen in flocks high up, scything through the air for insects.

Alpine Swift *Apus melba* 21cm

The largest swift to occur in the region, and easily told by its size and its white underparts with brown breast-band. One of its characteristic calls, heard from feeding flocks, is a loud, descending, chattering trill. Like other species of swift, it is thought to sleep in flight. It chooses its nest sites in rocky mountains, in sea cliffs and in old towns; the nest is a cup of plant material and feathers glued to a crevice with saliva. Mainly a summer visitor and passage migrant, breeding in Israel, Turkey, the east Mediterranean and south-west Arabia.

White-breasted Kingfisher *Halcyon smyrnensis* 26cm

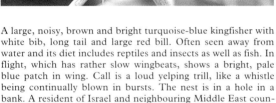

A large, noisy, brown and bright turquoise-blue kingfisher with white bib, long tail and large red bill. Often seen away from water and its diet includes reptiles and insects as well as fish. In flight, which has rather slow wingbeats, shows a bright, pale blue patch in wing. Call is a loud yelping trill, like a whistle being continually blown in bursts. The nest is in a hole in a bank. A resident of Israel and neighbouring Middle East countries, where it can be found by lakes and rivers and also in palm and olive groves.

Common Kingfisher *Alcedo atthis* 16cm

The flash of iridescent blue as this kingfisher flies along a river or the edge of a coastal estuary is an exciting experience. The smallest of the kingfishers to be found in Israel, the Common Kingfisher has a long bill, and is blue-green above and orange below, with a white chin and an orange flash behind the eye. A bird of rivers and lakes, but in winter also coastal areas. In the Middle East breeds only in Turkey, but birds move south in winter and occur down to the Mediterranean coasts and Arabian Gulf. Sometimes on migration can be found in the desert.

Pied Kingfisher *Ceryle rudis* 28cm

A conspicuous, unmistakable kingfisher with its large size and black and white plumage. The male has a double breast-band, while the female has a single one; feathers of the crown are elongated to form a short crest. Often seen perching in the open, and will hover and dive into water from a height to catch fish. Frequently occurs in small, loose groups. A resident of lakes and rivers in northern Israel, southern Turkey, Syria and the east Mediterranean.

Little Green Bee-eater *Merops orientalis* 25cm

The smallest bee-eater occurring in Israel and, unlike the two other species, it is a resident and most frequently seen in pairs. Green above and below, with copper-coloured underwing and a black stripe through eye. The race found in Israel has a blue throat. Occurs in open country with trees and cultivation, nesting in a tunnel made in a bank. Mainly a resident of Israel, Jordan and southern and eastern Arabia.

Blue-cheeked Bee-eater *Merops superciliosus* 30cm

Slightly larger than the European Bee-eater, and instantly told by its turquoise-green plumage with longer central tail feathers. Close views reveal a dark eye-stripe bordered by blue above and below, and a chestnut throat. Confusion is possible with the Little Green Bee-eater (both have rufous underwings), but that species is much smaller and lacks the chestnut on the throat. A breeding visitor to Israel, and is most likely to be seen in small flocks at the time of migration; fairly widespread on passage elsewhere in the Middle East.

European Bee-eater *Merops apiaster* 27cm

Similar in size to the Blue-cheeked Bee-eater, from which it is told by its chestnut crown and mantle, and yellow throat and lower back (Blue-cheeked is green, with blue, yellow and chestnut on the face). Both species occur in flocks, and their *proop proop* flight calls often indicate their presence overhead on migration. A summer visitor to its breeding grounds in Israel, Turkey, the east Mediterranean and parts of the Arabian Gulf, nesting colonially in holes in sandy banks.

European Roller *Coracias garrulus* 30cm

Rollers are large, colourful birds, being iridescent blue, black and chestnut. Their flight is rather slow, but when breeding they have a dramatic twisting and turning display flight, hence the name 'Roller'. Can be noisy, with a harsh, grating *krr krar* call, especially in flight. Occurs in open woods or farm-land with large trees, where it nests in holes. Often seen perched on telegraph wires on migration. A summer visitor to Israel and neigh-bouring countries; otherwise found on migration throughout the Middle East, though numbers have decreased in the past few decades.

Hoopoe *Upupa epops* 28cm

A familiar breeding bird and passage migrant throughout most of the region. Unmistakable with its pinkish-brown plumage, black and white wings and long, erectile crest. It can, however, be difficult to spot when feeding on the ground, and it is only when it flies that the full drama of its pattern can be appreciated. Song is a far-carrying *poo - poo - poo*. Occurs in open woodland, orchards and palm groves, nesting in a hole in a tree or building. Breeds in Israel, Turkey, east Mediterranean and parts of Arabia; widespread on migration.

Wryneck *Jynx torquilla* 16cm

This strange bird, related to the woodpeckers, has a most remarkable camouflaged plumage and a tendency to remain still, thus making it difficult to discover. The plumage is generally greyish, with a prominent black stripe on the head and back, a black stripe through the eye and a finely barred yellowish throat. Most likely to be observed on the ground when feeding on insects, particularly larvae. A spring and autumn migrant through the Middle East, including Israel, but never in flocks and nowhere common.

Syrian Woodpecker *Dendrocopos syriacus* 23cm

The only true woodpecker to occur in Israel, and identification should therefore not be a problem. Most people in Europe will be familiar with its close relative the Great Spotted Woodpecker (*Dendrocopos major*), found in the Middle East in high areas in Turkey; Syrian differs from Great Spotted in lacking a black bar joining the cheek stripe with the back of the head. Syrian Woodpeckers occur in woodlands, parks and olive groves in north and central Israel, throughout Turkey and in countries bordering the east Mediterranean. Nests in hole in tree which it usually excavates.

Bar-tailed Desert Lark *Ammomanes cincturus* 15cm

One of at least ten species of lark that breed in Israel. Most are rather similar, and good views are needed for correct identification. The Bar-tailed is rather plain and unstreaked, and most closely resembles the slightly larger Desert Lark, which can share the same semi-desert habitat; Bar-tailed, however, is much more of an open-desert or semi-desert species, and differs further from Desert Lark in its finer bill and clear-cut band to the tail. A breeding resident of southern Israel and scattered areas throughout the Middle East.

Desert Lark *Ammomanes deserti* 16cm

A rather featureless lark, similar in size to Skylark (*Alauda arvensis*). The bill is fairly heavy, with an orange-yellow base. Plumage varies depending on the local rock types, but is usually grey-buff, with slight streaking on breast, and with orange-brown tail with a broad, diffuse darker tip; birds on black lava deserts can be very dark. Inhabits arid, stony and rocky slopes and semi-deserts, often with scattered vegetation; frequently observed near human habitation. A resident of Israel and also, patchily, Arabia.

Hoopoe Lark *Alaemon alaudipes* 20cm

The tumbling song flight on outstretched black and white wings is one of the characteristic sights – and sounds – of the desert. On the ground, this is a rather large, upright lark with long, curved bill; its plumage looks pale sandy-buff, and at close range black spotting on the breast and black markings on the face may be noticed. When disturbed, will often run away quickly rather than fly. The song, heard mostly in the early morning, is a mournful series of flute-like notes accelerating towards the end. Mainly resident and widespread throughout the deserts and semi-deserts of southern Israel, Jordan, Syria and Arabia.

Calandra Lark *Melanocorypha calandra* 19cm

Richard Brooks; Windrush Photos

A large lark with stout head and bill and a black patch on side of neck, a feature it shares with Bimaculated Lark (*Melanocorypha bimaculata*). These two species are best separated in flight: Calandra has all-black wings below, with a white trailing edge; Bimaculated has paler underwings with no white trailing edge, and has a white tip to the tail. Calandra Lark is mainly a resident in central and northern Israel, as well as Turkey and the east Mediterranean, where it can be common on open cultivated and arable areas. Bimaculated Lark is a passage migrant through the Middle East, and in Israel a rare breeder in the north.

Short-toed Lark *Calandrella brachydactyla* 14cm

A small lark that gathers in large flocks, particularly on migration. As with all larks, it is a ground-dwelling bird that is often difficult to approach, as the whole flock will rise and move off to a safe distance. To identify a Short-toed Lark with certainty, one must see the pale breast with a dark mark at the side of the neck. When seen well, it is a perky bird, with crown feathers often raised and a pale flash above the eye. Breeds in open country, steppes, semi-deserts and plains in northern and western Israel, Turkey, Syria and Jordan; widespread in the Middle East on migration.

Crested Lark *Galerida cristata* 17cm

The commonest and tamest lark in Israel and the Middle East, and easily identified by its long pointed crest. In plumage it most closely resembles a Skylark (*Alauda arvensis*), but is greyer, with less bold streakings on the back; the bill is also more powerful than Skylark's. Musical song with slow, clear notes, in flight or perched. An abundant resident in Israel, often seen in pairs at the edge of tracks or roads, running swiftly from passing traffic; widespread elsewhere in the Middle East.

Temminck's Horned Lark *Eremophila bilopha* 14cm

Probably the most colourful lark of the desert. Told by its sandy upperparts and white underparts, with striking black and white face and breast pattern. Although the two species will not be encountered together, the Shore Lark (*Eremophila alpestris*), occurring in the mountains of northern Israel and Turkey, is rather similar; it is greyish above, with the face yellow and black (not white and black). Both have short 'horns' at the rear of the crown, and are fairly tame and easily approached. Temminck's Horned Lark is largely resident in the stony and sandy deserts of southern Israel, northern Arabia and adjacent Iraq, Syria and Jordan.

Sand Martin *Riparia riparia* 12cm

Alan Williams

This small martin is often found in flocks, both when breeding and on migration. The upperparts are brown and the underparts white, with a brown band across the breast. On migration, will often congregate with other martins and swallows. At its breeding grounds, it excavates a nesting burrow in sand pits or earth banks. A passage migrant through Israel to its Middle East breeding grounds in Turkey and north Syria.

85

Crag Martin *Ptyonoprogne rupestris* 14cm

Crag Martin   *African Rock Martin*

The Crag Martin and African Rock Martin (*Ptyonoprogne fuligula*), both illustrated, are very similar in appearance. The African Rock Martin, the smaller of the two species, is paler and greyer above and has paler underwing-coverts; the underparts are white, shading to pale grey, and the chin lacks the dark spotting of the Crag Martin. Both breed in Israel, the Crag Martin on Mount Hermon and the African Rock in the south and west. In the Middle East the Crag Martin is more northerly in its distribution, breeding mostly in the mountains of Turkey, whereas the African Rock Martin is confined to more southern areas of Arabia.

Barn Swallow *Hirundo rustica* 20cm

With its blue upperparts and long tail-streamers, can be confused only with Red-rumped Swallow, but is easily told by uniform upperparts (no pale rump) and red and blue on throat. During migration, often congregates in large flocks with martins to feed on insects, particularly over wetlands, where the birds roost communally in reedbeds and lakeside trees. Breeds in northern Israel and adjacent countries of the east Mediterranean, but is widespread on migration throughout the Middle East.

Red-rumped Swallow *Hirundo daurica* 17cm

Superficially resembles Barn Swallow (which see), but told by pale orange rump and nape, the latter dividing blue back from blue cap; the underparts are buffish-white. Also more leisurely in flight, with longer periods of gliding. Less prone to flocking than other swallows and martins, and frequently seen in pairs. The nest, which is cup-shaped with an entrance tunnel, is made of mud and sited under a bridge or in a building or cave. In the Middle East, it is a summer visitor to northern Israel and parts of the east Mediterranean, but resident in the mountains of south-west Arabia; found throughout the region on migration.

Tawny Pipit *Anthus campestris* 16.5cm

A fairly large, rather upright pipit, similar in size to a Yellow Wagtail. Sandy-buff plumage which, in adult, is almost unstreaked; young birds are lightly spotted or streaked on breast. It can be confused with Long-billed Pipit (which see) and also with Richard's Pipit (*Anthus richardi*), which is a scarce migrant and winter visitor to Israel. Richard's, however, is larger, with longer legs and heavier bill; it has dark streaks on the breast and on the mantle. Tawny Pipit is a summer visitor to its Middle East breeding grounds in Israel, Turkey and the east Mediterranean; found throughout the region on migration, especially in sparse grassland and semi-deserts.

Long-billed Pipit *Anthus similis* 17cm

Richard Porter

Very similar to Tawny Pipit, and it can be very difficult to distinguish between the two. The most helpful features to separate Long-billed from Tawny are its more upright stance, relatively shorter legs, greyer upperparts, buff (not white) outer tail feathers, and buff-orange lower underparts. When bird is perched, the tail is often flicked upwards and fanned outwards. Mainly resident in the highlands of north Israel, the east Mediterranean and south-west Arabia.

Red-throated Pipit *Anthus cervinus* 15cm

A small, streaked, brownish bird that frequents open grassland and the edges of pools and marshes, always on the ground. Easily told in summer plumage by its brick-red throat and upper breast. Otherwise heavily streaked brown, black and buff and thus very similar to the Meadow and Tree Pipit (*Anthus pratensis* and *A. trivialis*) that are also found on migration and in winter in Israel. Often occurs in small flocks and, when flushed, has a very high, thin *speeee* flight call. The Red-throated Pipit does not breed in the Middle East, but occurs widely on migration.

Yellow Wagtail *Motacilla flava* 16.5cm

The Yellow Wagtail complex comprises a number of races, four of which are recorded commonly in Israel on migration. The males can be differentiated by their head colour and pattern, and one of the commonest in Israel has a glossy black head – the so-called Black-headed Wagtail, illustrated here. This occurs widely on migration and is the only race to breed in the Middle East. The other races, all of which occur throughout the region on passage, have head colour varying from all yellow to all dark grey, with or without a white stripe over the eye. They occur mainly on flat grassland near water.

(Above) male Black-headed race; (below) female

Citrine Wagtail *Motacilla citreola* 18cm

In summer plumage, the male is easily recognized by its bright yellow head and underparts, contrasting with grey back; it is thus one of the most distinctive wagtails. The female and young birds are far less distinct and can be confused with Yellow or White Wagtails; the female can be told by its greyish upperparts and yellow on face, which extends around the ear-coverts, while young have the same face pattern but lack the yellow. A regular passage migrant to Israel, but rare elsewhere in the Middle East.

Grey Wagtail *Motacilla cinerea* 18cm

Superficially resembles a Yellow Wagtail, but this is a bird found almost entirely on watercourses and fast-running streams. It has a longer tail than the Yellow Wagtail, an entirely grey back, with dark wings, and the male, in summer, has a black throat. Never seen in flocks (as Yellow Wagtails often are), and has rather exaggerated movements of its body and tail when feeding at a stream edge. Has a high-pitched metallic call which often first attracts one to it. In the Middle East breeds only on hill streams in Turkey, but is widespread on migration and in winter throughout the region, including Israel.

White Wagtail *Motacilla alba* 17.5cm

The pied plumage with grey back and long, frequently wagged tail easily identify this active, ground-dwelling species. In slightly undulating flight, frequently utters a melodious *cher-it* call. Juvenile birds are much plainer grey, and the head markings are just a shadow of those shown by the adult. White Wagtails are found in most open habitats, but especially on flat areas near water. Nests in ruins, bridges, and crevices in buildings. In the Middle East, breeds in Turkey and parts of the east Mediterranean, including northern Israel (but rare); widespread and common throughout the region on migration and in winter, often roosting in large dense flocks on trees or buildings.

Yellow-vented Bulbul *Pycnonotus xanthopygos* 19cm

One of the typical birds of well-vegetated areas of Israel, as well as the east Mediterranean, southern Turkey and Arabia. Like a small thrush with fairly long tail and 'floppy' actions. The sooty head and throat merge into the grey upperparts and pale grey underparts; the tail is blackish. Note especially the white eye-ring and yellow undertail-coverts. Fairly tame and noisy, the characteristic song and call notes have a fluty quality that is easily remembered: *bly-bly-bly-bly*. A resident in most places with trees, bushes and scrub; can be found in palm groves and the centres of towns.

Grey Hypocolius *Hypocolius ampelinus* 23cm

Superficially, this Middle East endemic resembles a slim Southern Grey Shrike, but has a longer black-tipped tail and shorter wings which do not show any black when perched. In far-ranging flight, note the male's black primaries with prominent white tips and long tail. In winter, parties will circle around high for several minutes. The world breeding range is confined to Iran and Iraq, birds moving south in winter to Saudi Arabia, Bahrain (where very large flocks can occur) and other parts of the Arabian Gulf; in Israel, however, it is a rare migrant, mainly to the Eilat area.

Dunnock *Prunella modularis* 14cm

An unobtrusive grey-brown, largely ground-dwelling bird. It superficially resembles a sparrow, but the rufous-brown upperparts are dark-streaked and the head and underparts largely greyish. The bill is fine, not chunky like a sparrow's. On the ground, it progresses with shuffling and rather jerky movements. Migrant Dunnocks from breeding grounds in Europe and Asia reach Israel and neighbouring parts of the Middle East in winter, but this species is never common.

Radde's Accentor *Prunella ocularis* 15cm

Richard Porter

Generally similar in shape and behaviour to Dunnock, but told by the striking head pattern: blackish crown and cheeks and broad white stripe above the eye. A winter visitor to the hills of northern Israel and nearby areas of the Middle East, these birds almost certainly coming from breeding grounds in eastern Turkey. The much rarer Black-throated Accentor (*Prunella atrogularis*), a rare winter visitor to Israel, is similar to Radde's, but can instantly be separated by the small black throat patch which most birds show.

92

Rufous Bush Robin *Cercotrichas galactotes* 15.5cm

The most noticeable feature of the Rufous Bush Robin, which is the size of a small thrush, is its rufous tail with broad white tips to the feathers. Especially obvious below, these can be observed most readily when the bird raises and spreads its tail, which it does frequently. Otherwise, a pale grey brown bird with pale stripe above the eye and pale fringes to the wing feathers. Occurs in rather open, dry country with scrub, olive groves and prickly pear. A breeding summer visitor to Israel and neighbouring countries of the Middle East; on migration, it is found throughout the region.

Black Bush Robin *Cercotrichas podobe* 21cm

Resembles a small Blackbird, but with long legs and with long, graduated tail that is frequently held cocked, especially when singing or just after alighting on a bush top. Characteristic white fringes to undertail-coverts and tips of tail feathers below, especially noticeable as tail is swept upwards. A bird of sandy plains with bushes and low tangled vegetation, and most often seen in pairs. Resident in southern Arabia, but the population is expanding northwards and now starting to be found in Israel and may even have bred there.

Thrush Nightingale *Luscinia luscinia* 16cm

The Thrush Nightingale and Common Nightingale (*Luscinia megarhynchos*) are very similar. Both resemble a small thrush with brownish upperparts and rusty-coloured tail. Thrush Nightingale (illustrated), which is the duller of the two species, has distinct mottling on its greyish breast, whereas the Common Nightingale has clean greyish-white underparts. Both are very skulking and difficult to see. The Common Nightingale is a breeding summer visitor to northern Israel, where it is best located by its striking, rich, musical song. The Thrush Nightingale occurs only on migration and is far less common.

Bluethroat *Luscinia svecica* 14cm

(Above) adult; (below) juvenile

A Robin-sized bird, the male of which is very easily told in breeding plumage by its blue bib with an orange or white spot in the centre. Females and males in winter are less obvious, but look for the reddish sides to the tail base, a white stripe above the eye and a blackish necklace. Mainly a ground-dwelling bird, most often seen near water and swampy areas with thick vegetation and reeds. A common passage migrant and winter visitor to Israel and other areas of the Middle East, though in the region only breeds in eastern Turkey.

White-throated Robin *Irania gutturalis* 16.5cm

The white throat of the male can be very difficult to see unless the bird is facing you; the most noticeable features are the black sides of face, white stripe above eye, orange breast and black tail. The rather drab female has an orange wash to sides of breast and a black tail. Spends much time on the ground, where it seeks out the densest cover. Tail frequently cocked. A summer visitor, breeding in Turkey and the east Mediterranean countries, including northern Israel (where local), on stony hillsides and valleys with scrub, where its loud, clear song is the best indicator of its presence; otherwise scarce on migration throughout the Middle East.

Black Redstart *Phoenicurus ochruros* 14cm

Male identified by smoky-grey upperparts, black breast, deep red lower breast and belly, and reddish tail which is frequently quivered; the extent of red on lower breast can vary. The similar Common Redstart (*Phoenicurus phoenicurus*) has a white forehead, black confined to chin and throat, and pale grey upperparts. Both species may show a white flash in the wing. The females of the two are less easy to separate, but female Black Redstarts are more dusky grey in coloration. In the Middle East, largely a summer visitor to its breeding grounds in the mountains of

Richard Porter

Turkey, Syria and northern Israel; common on migration and in winter throughout much of the region, including Israel.

95

Blackstart *Cercomela melanura* 15cm

A rather featureless smoky grey chat with an all-black tail, which is frequently spread outwards in conjunction with the half-spreading of its wings. Usually seen in pairs – male and female have similar plumage – in rocky wadis or the edges of deserts with scattered bushes, where it is often one of the most characteristic species. Has a melancholy song of short, deep, flute-like phrases and whistles, and often allows a close approach. A resident of Israel, Jordan and the Red Sea coastlands.

Stonechat *Saxicola torquata* 12.5cm

The handsome male Stonechat, with its round head, short tail and perky movements, especially its constantly flicking tail, is most likely to be seen perched prominently on bush tops. It is easily told by its blackish head and orange underparts, with a conspicuous, white half neck-band. The female has drab brownish, streaked head and upperparts and a faint orange wash on the breast. Stonechats have a patchy distribution, breeding in Turkey and southern Arabia; in winter and on migration, found throughout most of the Middle East, including Israel.

A very upright, pale wheatear of the plains. It is one of the largest wheatears of the Middle East, similar in size to the Red-breasted Wheatear (*Oenanthe bottae*) of the mountain plateaux of south-west Arabia. Most easily confused with the female or immature of the Northern Wheatear (*Oenanthe oenanthe*): note its larger size, more upright stance, longer legs and paler, more uniform grey-buff plumage; the tail also has a broader dark terminal band. The sexes are similar in plumage. A bird of open plains, semi-deserts and stony steppes. In the Middle East, breeds in Turkey and scattered parts of Israel, Syria, Jordan and Lebanon; otherwise occurs extensively on migration throughout the region.

Cyprus Pied Wheatear *Oenanthe cypriaca* 14cm

Like all wheatears, this is mostly a ground-dwelling bird. In summer, the male has black back connecting with black throat and sides of neck, features that distinguish it from the Black-eared Wheatear (which does not breed in Cyprus). Confusable with Pied Wheatear (*Oenanthe pleschanka*), but differs in warmer buff breast and slightly broader black tail-band; in general, outside Cyprus, the two species are inseparable (Pied Wheatear is a widespread migrant throughout the Middle East, but is not illustrated in this book). Breeds only on the island of Cyprus, on stony hillsides with scattered bushes; its wintering areas are uncertain, but it is found in Israel on migration.

Black-eared Wheatear *Oenanthe hispanica* 15cm

Females of all the wheatears are difficult to identify, and this should not be attempted by the beginner. It is best to concentrate first on the males. The male Black-eared has two types, one with a black throat and the other with a black patch through the eye; both have pale sandy back and black wings. Note the white rump and white sides of the tail, typical of most wheatears. A bird of open rocky or lightly wooded country with scattered vegetation, but on migration also cultivated fields and semi-deserts. A summer visitor to northern Israel, Lebanon and Turkey; on migration, found throughout much of the Middle East.

Desert Wheatear *Oenanthe deserti* 14cm

(Above) male; (below) female

Despite its name, the Desert Wheatear is largely a winter visitor to most parts of the Middle East. It differs from the other wheatears in the region in its all-black tail and buffish-white rump. Otherwise a sandy-buff wheatear with black wings which, on the male, join up with a black or blackish throat. Occurs in sandy or gravel steppes and semi-deserts, both in its breeding areas and on migration. Mainly resident in its breeding areas in parts of Israel and nearby Middle East countries; also a passage migrant and winter visitor to much of the Middle East except Turkey and Cyprus, where rare.

Hooded Wheatear *Oenanthe monacha* 17cm

The largest wheatear to occur in Israel, having long tail, wings and bill. The male is a very smart black and white bird, with the black of the head extending well down the breast and just black corners to the white tail (no black tail-band). The female is sandy-brown with a buffish (not white) rump and sides of tail, which, like the male's, lacks a black terminal band. Has a unique, buoyant, butterfly-like flight when catching aerial insects. A resident of southern Israel and isolated areas of the Middle East, inhabiting rocky ravines and deserts.

(Above) male; (below) female

White-crowned Black Wheatear *Oenanthe leucopyga* 17cm

A large wheatear which is all black with a white crown, white rump and tail (except for black central tail feathers) and white undertail-coverts. On young birds the crown is all black, as it is on some females. The other large wheatear in Israel is the much rarer Hooded, the male of which has white underparts up to the breast and more extensive white on the head. A resident of southern Israel, with a patchy distribution also in northern Saudi Arabia, occurring in rocky deserts and even around settlements.

Rock Thrush *Monticola saxatilis* 19cm

The size of a small thrush with long bill and short tail, characters shown by all the rock thrushes. The male is quite striking with its blue-grey and rusty-red plumage and an unexpected white panel on back. The female is similar to female Blue Rock Thrush, but paler, with pale-spotted upperparts (plain on Blue Rock) and rusty-red tail (dark brown on Blue Rock). Unlike the Blue Rock Thrush, this is a summer visitor to the Middle East, where it breeds in the mountains of northern Israel and Turkey.

Blue Rock Thrush *Monticola solitarius* 20cm

The male is similar in size to a Blackbird and is, as its name implies, dark blue. It may be shy and difficult to approach, and is most frequently seen perching on a rock in a prominent position. The female is dull brown, barred and spotted below. Mountain ranges, cliff faces and rocky deserts are the breeding areas, but has a wide range of habitats on migration and in winter. A resident in northern and central Israel and scattered areas in the east Mediterranean; otherwise a migrant and winter visitor to most parts of the Middle East.

Blackbird *Turdus merula* 24cm

The male is all black, with a yellow bill and yellow eye-ring. A familiar bird to those living in Europe, but less so in the Middle East. The female and young males are all dark brown, with yellowish or dark bill. Seen both in trees and on the ground, where it runs in short bursts, stopping to look for food – worms are a particular favourite. A bird of woodlands, gardens and plantations. In the Middle East, breeds in northern Israel, adjacent countries of the east Mediterranean and Turkey.

Fan-tailed Cisticola *Cisticola juncidis* 10cm

Alan Williams

A small warbler that is seen and identified mostly in flight, which is undulating and wide-ranging over grass, cereal crops or reed tops. Then, its characteristic song, a rhythmically repeated, almost metallic *pzit*, alerts you to its presence. When perched, it is a buffish warbler with bold dark streaking on its back; note also the white tips to the short tail when seen from below. Typically found in grain fields, grassy meadows and along the edges of marshes. Largely resident, with a patchy distribution in northern Israel and adjacent countries of the east Mediterranean, as well as parts of southern Arabia.

Graceful Prinia *Prinia gracilis* 10cm

A rather indistinct small, grey-buff warbler with a long tail that is constantly waved up and down and from side to side. Close views reveal a reddish-brown eye and lightly streaked upperparts. Difficult to get a good view of as it is always very active, but the song is distinctive and often the first indication of its presence: a monotonous, rhythmic *ze-vit…ze-vit…ze-vit….* A bird of scrub and low vegetation, and often found in villages and towns. A common resident in Israel and many coastal areas of the Middle East.

Scrub Warbler *Scotocerca inquieta* 10cm

A small, perky, ground-dwelling bird. Superficially similar to the Graceful Prinia, but its actions are quite distinct. Note the chunky body, large head with dark stripe through the eye and pale line above, and also the long tail cocked high as it hops on the ground, rather secretively and never far from cover. Occurs on stony hillsides and in semi-deserts with low scrub, often in mountains. A resident of Israel and parts of Arabia.

Moustached Warbler *Acrocephalus melanopogon* 13cm

Richard Brooks

Very similar to the much commoner Sedge Warbler, another species that is found in reedbeds. A warm buff-brown bird with streaked upperparts, noticeable white stripe above the eye and dark crown. The Sedge Warbler has a buffish-white stripe above the eye and is paler above. Note the Moustached Warbler's habit of holding its tail raised (rarely shown by Sedge Warbler). Occurs in reedbeds and swamps, nesting in reeds or bushes above shallow water. Has a patchy Middle East distribution in northern Israel, the east Mediterranean countries and northern Arabia; more widespread on passage and in winter.

Sedge Warbler *Acrocephalus schoenobaenus* 13cm

This wetland warbler is most likely to be confused with the Moustached Warbler, both having streaked upperparts and a conspicuous whitish stripe above the eye. The Sedge, however, is paler above (Moustached is more reddish-brown), with paler, streaked crown (blackish on Moustached). The call is a hard *tchek* and also a fast churring *trrr*. A bird of reedbeds and overgrown wet areas, but also in bushes away from water on migration. In Israel it is a passage migrant, as it is throughout most of the Middle East.

103

European Reed Warbler *Acrocephalus scirpaceus* 13cm

A plain brownish warbler found almost entirely in reedbeds. Close views reveal a rusty tone to the rump, buff underparts, a pale line above the eye, rather flat crown and a rounded tail. It is thus similar to Marsh Warbler (*Acrocephalus palustris*), and separation of the two is not advised unless heard singing: European Reed Warbler has a monotonous, grating song on much the same pitch, whereas that of Marsh Warbler is musical, liquid and varied. The former is a summer visitor to Israel, where it nests in reedy areas. Marsh Warbler does not breed in the Middle East, but is widespread on passage.

Clamorous Reed Warbler *Acrocephalus stentoreus* 18cm

One of the two largest warblers to occur in the region, the other being the very similar Great Reed Warbler (*Acrocephalus arundinaceus*). A summer visitor to the east Mediterranean and Turkey. Essentially it is a large brownish warbler of reedbeds, as is the Great Reed Warbler. Both are almost the size of a thrush, and separation of the two should not be attempted by inexperienced observers. They have similar loud, raucous songs. A breeding resident of reedbeds in Israel and other areas of the Middle East, where it also nests in mangroves on the Red Sea coast.

Olivaceous Warbler *Hippolais pallida* 12cm

A medium-sized warbler that is difficult to identify. As it is one of the commonest breeding warblers in northern areas of the Middle East and fairly common on migration, however, we have included it. You need to 'get your eye in' with warblers. The Olivaceous is olive-brown above with a slight greyish wash, and has a rather indistinct pale line above the eye; the underparts are buffish-white, with a white throat. The bill is fairly large, brown with a flesh-coloured lower mandible; the legs are greyish. On the breeding grounds listen for its rhythmic, energetic song. A summer visitor to its breeding areas in Israel, Turkey and the Near East; otherwise occurs on migration throughout the Middle East.

Upcher's Warbler *Hippolais languida* 14cm

Similar to the Olivaceous Warbler but slightly larger, with a rounder head and crown peaking in front of the eye; these details, however, are rather subtle. Best told by its dark tail, which is waved in a rather uncoordinated way; this is especially noticeable after the bird has just alighted. Upperparts are brownish-grey, and the wings usually have a pale panel. Generally a bird of scrub in plains and mountain valleys, but on migration also in acacia and tamarisk scrub. A summer visitor to northern Israel, southern Turkey, Syria and Lebanon; on migration, occurs throughout the Middle East, but is scarce.

Olive-tree Warbler *Hippolais olivetorum* 15cm

A large, greyish-brown warbler with an obvious pale wing panel and heavy, yellowish bill. These features distinguish it from all other warblers, although good views are required as many members of the warbler family are difficult to identify. In the Middle East, it is a breeding summer visitor to the olive groves and oak woodlands of Turkey and Syria, passing through Israel and neighbouring parts of the region on passage, but it is never commonly seen.

Spectacled Warbler *Sylvia conspicillata* 13cm

A small warbler, similar to the Whitethroat, but smaller, shorter-tailed and brighter. The most noticeable feature is the rusty-red wing, shown by both males and females. Compared with Whitethroat, has a darker grey head, almost blackish in front of and around the eye. A bird of low scrub, in which it moves restlessly; also frequently seen hopping on the ground. The rattling *trrrrr* call note is often the first indication of its presence. In the Middle East, largely confined to Israel, Jordan and Cyprus, where it is mostly resident.

Subalpine Warbler *Sylvia cantillans* 12cm

A small warbler of scrubby hillsides, the male of which is easily identified by its ash-grey upperparts, deep reddish-orange underparts and noticeable white moustache. Close views reveal a red eye-ring. The song, from bush top or in song flight, is fast and scratchy with clear and musical phrases. In the Middle East, breeds in low scrub, thickets and open woodland in western Turkey, where it is a summer visitor; in Israel it is a scarce passage migrant, as it is in most countries of the region.

Ménétries's Warbler *Sylvia mystacea* 12cm

An active warbler of scrub and small trees which is very similar to the Sardinian Warbler. Separation of the females of the two species is extremely difficult, but the male Ménétries's is told from the male Sardinian by its black forehead and ear-coverts merging into its grey-brown upperparts (black head not clear-cut as on Sardinian); note also the pinkish wash on breast and throat demarcating the white moustache. The slightly shorter tail is frequently waved. Occurs in scrub, bushes on river edges and gardens. In the Middle East, breeds in eastern Turkey, parts of Iraq and Syria, where it is a summer visitor; more widespread in the region on passage, but rare in Israel.

Sardinian Warbler *Sylvia melanocephala* 13cm

The male Sardinian Warbler is easily told by its shiny black head contrasting with white throat, grey body and noticeable red ring around the eye. See Ménétries's Warbler for further distinctions. An active bird, with tail often held cocked, and its presence often indicated by its frequent rattling, churring call note. The females of the 'scrub warblers' are very similar and not easily distinguishable by novice birdwatchers. Occurs in dry, bushy country, as well as in pine and evergreen-oak forests. In the Middle East, breeds in Israel and neighbouring countries, including western Turkey, where it is a partial migrant; more widespread in the region in winter.

Cyprus Warbler *Sylvia melanothorax* 13cm

(Above) male; (below) female

Found breeding only in Cyprus. The male is easily told by its white underparts marked with black bars and streakings, demarcated from the greyish upperparts by a white moustache – the only warbler to show such markings. The female is similar to female Sardinian Warbler, but usually shows dark crescent-shaped markings on throat and breast, as well as white moustachial stripe. A resident and partial migrant in Cyprus, where it breeds on rocky slopes with shrubs; otherwise a winter visitor to Israel and neighbouring countries, where it usually occurs in dry wadis and acacia woodland.

Rüppell's Warbler *Sylvia rueppelli* 14cm

One of the easiest warblers to identify, by its black head and throat with prominent white moustache. The female is duller but still shows a white moustache, though the head and throat are often mottled. Where it occurs on its breeding grounds, can be quite common. A summer visitor to the Middle East, arriving at the end of March in southern and western Turkey, where it breeds in low scrub and bushes; on migration, found in Israel and neighbouring countries, especially favouring acacia woodland.

Arabian Warbler *Sylvia leucomelaena* 14.5cm

A large warbler which is one of the specialities of the Middle East. Most easily confused with the Orphean Warbler (*Sylvia hortensis*), but note the shorter wings, longer black tail with just white fringes at the sides, and dark eyes. Differs also in its habit of flopping its tail downwards or in a circular movement. Has a pleasant, loud warbling song, often the first indication of its presence. A resident warbler occurring largely in dry acacia woodland in Israel, Jordan and along the edge of the Red Sea.

Barred Warbler *Sylvia nisoria* 15cm

A large warbler with slow, heavy movements. In breeding plumage the male, with its white underparts barred with dark crescents, is unmistakable; note also the pale yellow iris, which gives a staring expression. The female is similar, but markings are less distinct. Young birds are not barred, but rather sandy-greyish; they can be told by their large size, rather lumbering movements, pale fringes to the wing feathers and dark fringes to the undertail-coverts. A bird of scattered trees which on migration it is found throughout the Middle East, including Israel.

Lesser Whitethroat *Sylvia curruca* 13.5cm

This species comprises several very similar subspecies (some of which are often considered to be full species in their own right). The Lesser Whitethroat illustrated here breeds in Turkey and parts of the east Mediterranean, including northern Israel; it occurs on migration throughout much of the Middle East and even winters in southern Arabia. Note the grey plumage with a dark mask through the eye, absence of any rufous in the wing and dark legs. The much paler Desert Lesser Whitethroat (form *minula*), a winter visitor to Arabia, has a washed-out appearance. Hume's Lesser Whitethroat (form *althaea*) is darker and stouter; it is an uncommon winter visitor to the Arabian Gulf.

Whitethroat *Sylvia communis* 14cm

A common, medium-sized warbler of scrub and bushy habitats, most closely resembling Spectacled Warbler and Lesser Whitethroat. It differs from the Spectacled Warbler in its larger size, longer tail, more uniformly grey head and less rufous wings; from Lesser Whitethroat in rufous wings, orange legs, whiter eye-ring and more evenly grey head. The short song, often uttered in dancing song flight, is a scratchy warbling. A breeding summer visitor to Israel (and areas to the north) and passage migrant throughout the Middle East.

Blackcap *Sylvia atricapilla* 14cm

One of the commonest warblers to be seen in much of the Middle East, mostly on passage. On its breeding grounds it is a fine songster. The male is easily told by its jet-black cap, as are the female and young birds by their reddish-brown cap. The Garden Warbler (*Sylvia borin*), which is also found on migration in the region, though less commonly, is similar, but lacks the black or brown cap. In the Middle East, a summer visitor to the woodlands mainly of northern Turkey; otherwise a passage migrant through the region, including Israel.

(Above) male; (below) female

Eastern Bonelli's Warbler *Phylloscopus orientalis* 11cm

Bonelli's Warbler has recently been split into Western and Eastern Bonelli's. Both species are similar to the Chiffchaff and Willow Warbler, and close views are needed for identification. Similar in size to Chiffchaff, but the plumage is greyish above and whitish below, with a plain face; note the green edgings to the wing, tail feathers and the greenish rump. The song is a characteristic trill and the call a short *chip*. A summer visitor to its Middle East breeding grounds in western and southern Turkey and isolated areas in Syria; occurs on migration in the east Mediterranean, including Israel.

Willow Warbler *Phylloscopus trochilus* 11.5cm

This small, active, olive-coloured warbler is most easily confused with the Chiffchaff, which is also a common migrant in Israel. Some birds are almost impossible to separate, but note the Willow Warbler's pale legs (dark on Chiffchaff), slightly longer wings and more yellowish appearance, especially of young birds in the autumn. The call, which is frequently uttered, is a soft *hu-eet*, slightly more disyllabic than that of Chiffchaff. Willow Warblers do not breed in the Middle East, but are common on migration in Israel and throughout the region; they can occur in any area with trees.

112

Chiffchaff *Phylloscopus collybita* 11cm

The Chiffchaff and Willow Warbler are very similar and are the two commonest 'leaf warblers' in the region. The Chiffchaff is the smaller of the two and a rather drab grey-green, with generally less yellow in the plumage. It has dark legs, whereas the Willow Warbler has pale legs. Both have a similar *hoo-eet* call note, but the Chiffchaff's is almost monosyllabic. Although it is found breeding in the Middle East only in northern and western Turkey, where it is a summer visitor to woodlands, it occurs on migration or as a winter visitor throughout the region, including Israel.

Spotted Flycatcher *Muscicapa striata* 14cm

Flycatchers have a characteristic flight: upwards from their perch and manoeuvring in erratic circles for flying insects, then returning usually to the same perch. The Spotted Flycatcher is a brownish bird above, with pale streaks on the forehead and pale fringes to the wing feathers; below, it is whitish with a streaked breast. Breeds in parks, woodland edges and plantations, nesting on ledges in buildings or on a branch against a tree trunk. In the Middle East, it is a summer visitor to Turkey and parts of the east Mediterranean, including northern Israel, but occurs throughout the region on migration.

113

Red-breasted Flycatcher *Ficedula parva* 12cm

Richard Porter

In summer plumage, the male is easily told by its red breast – almost Robin-like, but its behaviour is quite different. The rest of the plumage is grey-brown, with white underparts, and a black tail with white sides at the base. The female and young birds lack the red breast. Active and perky, with tail often held cocked, but can easily disappear into the cover of trees and not be obvious. In the Middle East, a summer visitor to isolated areas of northern Turkey, where it breeds in deciduous forests; otherwise a rather rare migrant in the east Mediterranean, including Israel.

Collared Flycatcher *Ficedula albicollis* 13cm

Richard Brooks; Windrush Photos

A black and white flycatcher: black above and white below, with a large white patch in the wing and white collar around the neck. The female, young birds and winter-plumaged males are brown above, white below, with a small white wing patch. The other similar species occurring in the Middle East are the Pied and Semi-collared Flycatchers (*Ficedula hypoleuca* and *F. semitorquata*), and on autumn migration, when they are not in breeding plumage, distinguishing between the three is very difficult. All are passage migrants through the east Mediterranean, including Israel.

114

Arabian Babbler *Turdoides squamiceps* 26cm

A large, noisy, thrush-like bird with a long tail. The plumage is grey-brown, with fine, dark streaks on upperparts and breast. It spends much time on the ground, where it hops with tail raised, and usually occurs in small groups which fly from bush to bush in 'follow-my-leader' fashion. This resident species is found only in the Middle East, frequenting dry, scrubby areas, especially with acacias, from Israel south along the coasts of the Red and Arabian Seas up to the Arabian Gulf.

Sombre Tit *Parus lugubris* 14cm

A large, rather drab-plumaged tit with dull black-brown cap, throat and upper breast. Upperparts greyish and underparts off-white. Tends to spend its time low to the ground or among rocks, searching for food. Rarely gathers in flocks as other members of the tit family commonly do. Occurs in plains and on mountain slopes with rocky outcrops and scrub, nesting in hole in tree or rock; it can also be attracted to nestboxes. In the Middle East, a resident breeding bird in Turkey and parts of the east Mediterranean, including the slopes of Mount Hermon in northern Israel.

115

Great Tit *Parus major* 14cm

Where it occurs, the Great Tit is one of the commonest and most obvious birds of woodland. A large tit with black cap, white cheeks, and yellow underparts with a broad black stripe down the centre. Young birds are duller, with yellowish cheeks. It has a wide range of calls based around a typical ringing and pleasant *chee-tweede-a-weet*. Will often gather in small flocks outside the breeding season. Nests in hole in tree. A resident of northern Israel and neighbouring east Mediterranean countries, including Turkey and Cyprus.

Western Rock Nuthatch *Sitta neumayer* 14cm

Two species of rock nuthatch occur in the Middle East. The Western Rock Nuthatch is the commoner, but in Israel it is found only on the higher slopes of Mount Hermon. The larger Eastern (or Great) Rock Nuthatch (*Sitta tephronota*) is confined to a small area of south-east Turkey and does not occur in Israel. The two species are very similar. Note the pale grey upperparts, whitish underparts (with orange wash on undertail-coverts) and black stripe through the eye. The Western Rock Nuthatch frequents rocky gorges, mountains and cliffs, where its nest is a mud construction with a tunnel entrance, usually under overhanging rock. In addition to northern Israel, it is a resident of Turkey, Lebanon and Syria.

Wallcreeper *Tichodroma muraria* 17cm

As it hops up and along the wall of a cliff, rock face, or amongst boulders searching for insects, the Wallcreeper can appear a rather drab greyish bird – but then it will flick its wings half-open to reveal a flash of crimson. This becomes even more noticeable in flight, especially as the broad, rounded, crimson wings are adorned with white spots near the wingtip. Breeds in rocky ravines and ruins up to the snow-line in parts of Turkey; in winter, some birds move south to reach Israel, Cyprus and other parts of the east Mediterranean. Nowhere is it common and patience is needed to find it.

Penduline Tit *Remiz pendulinus* 11cm

A small bird of the trees of wetland fringes. Rather pale, with a characteristic black mask through the eye and a chestnut back. The bird's presence is often indicated by its thin, high *tsee* call, or else by the sight of its nest hanging over water from the branches of a tree, especially willow. Breeds in reedbeds and trees near wetlands in Turkey and Syria, building a suspended oval-shaped nest with an entrance tube at the side; in autumn birds disperse south, reaching most of Israel, Cyprus and parts of northern Arabia.

Windrush Photos

117

Palestine Sunbird *Nectarinia osea* 11cm

Male   *Female*

The commonest and most familiar sunbird in the Middle East, and the only one to be found in Israel. A small, very active bird with a fairly long, decurved bill. The male in breeding plumage is blue-black with a metallic sheen which, in some lights, can appear green. If you are very lucky, you will see orange tufts at the sides of the breast. Females and young birds are grey-brown with paler underparts. Like all sunbirds, it feeds on the nectar of flowers. A resident of the Middle East, the only region of the world in which it occurs, inhabiting well-vegetated areas from Israel and Lebanon south along the Red Sea coast, through Yemen to Oman.

Golden Oriole *Oriolus oriolus* 24cm

Gordon Langsbury; Windrush Photos

A thrush-sized bird found where there are large trees. The male is unmistakable with its golden-yellow plumage and black wings, but can often be hard to see within the tree canopy, until it flies. The female is less distinct, being yellowish-green in coloration. In flight, which is fast, note the long, gentle undulations, somewhat reminiscent of a woodpecker. The song is a mellow, fluty *too-lee-too-lee*, easily remembered once heard. A summer visitor to the Middle East and can be seen on passage throughout; it breeds in Turkey, Cyprus and northern Syria, and occasionally in isolated areas in Israel and northern Saudi Arabia.

Isabelline Shrike *Lanius isabellinus* 18cm

A pale shrike, similar to the Red-backed Shrike, but with longer tail and more sandy-coloured plumage. Both sexes at all ages have a rusty tail, which is the most diagnostic feature; adults also show rather greyish upperparts and a black mask. Its usual preference is for dry country with scattered bushes and trees, especially acacias. Does not breed in the Middle East, but occurs on migration from Asia throughout much of the region, although rare in Israel and Turkey.

Red-backed Shrike *Lanius collurio* 17cm

The shrikes are known as 'butcher birds', because they often impale the insects and small animals (including birds) that they catch on thorns in a favourite tree. This is known as their 'larder'. The male Red-backed has a blue-grey head contrasting with reddish-brown back and a black mask through the eye. The female is duller, with just a faint mask through the eye and dark scallop-shaped marks on the whitish underparts. A summer visitor to its Middle East breeding grounds in Turkey and parts of the east Mediterranean, including northern Israel; otherwise a fairly common passage migrant in spring and autumn throughout the region.

(Above) male; (below) female

119

Lesser Grey Shrike *Lanius minor* 20cm

Very similar to the Southern Grey Shrike and care needed to separate the two, especially in spring and autumn, when they both occur on migration. The Lesser Grey is best told by the broad black band across its forehead (forehead grey on Southern Grey) and pink wash on underparts; it also has proportionately longer wings and shorter tail than Southern Grey. At times of migration, shrikes are one of the typical birds of roadside telegraph wires, and close views can often be obtained. A migrant through Israel and other parts of the Middle East, but breeds only in Turkey.

Southern Grey Shrike *Lanius meridionalis* 26cm

Richard Porter

Very like the Great Grey Shrike (*Lanius excubitor*) of northern Europe, and only recently 'split' from that species by taxonomists. Note its grey upperparts, white underparts, and prominent black markings: black mask through the eye, and black wings and tail. It is told from the very similar Lesser Grey Shrike by larger size, shorter wings and grey forehead. A breeding bird of much of Israel, the east Mediterranean (except Turkey) and parts of Arabia; birds breeding in Asia migrate to the region in winter.

Woodchat Shrike *Lanius senator* 17cm

A very distinctive shrike in adult plumage with its chestnut head, black back and tail and large white wing patches. In flight, note the white rump. Young birds are more difficult to identify, being rather similar to young Red-backed and Masked Shrikes; best told from Red-backed by their creamy shoulder patches and rump. A fine songster, with clear whistles and much imitation of other birds. A summer visitor to open country with trees in northern Israel, neighbouring east Mediterranean countries and south and west Turkey; occurs on migration throughout the Middle East.

Masked Shrike *Lanius nubicus* 18cm

The adult, with its black and white plumage and orange-yellow wash on the sides of the underparts, is a handsome bird. It has a longer-tailed appearance than the other shrikes. The young birds are not easy to distinguish from young Woodchat Shrikes (both have whitish shoulder patches), but they are greyer, less brown, with longer tail and finer bill. The Masked Shrike's world breeding range is almost entirely confined to the Middle East: it is a summer visitor to northern Israel, neighbouring east Mediterranean countries and south and west Turkey; on spring and autumn migration found throughout the Middle East, and a few winter in south-west Arabia.

121

Jay *Garrulus glandarius* 34cm

The most colourful member of the crow family, though probably the shyest. It is especially striking in flight, when it reveals blue and white patches on broad wings, and white rump contrasting with a rather short black tail. When seen close, note the stout bill, which is particularly adept at dealing with acorns, one of its main food items. The flight is slow, with quite deep undulations. Jays are heard more often than seen: the far-carrying, harsh cry often indicates their presence in coniferous or deciduous woodland, in which they are resident in northern Israel and areas north to Turkey.

Magpie *Pica pica* 48cm

A well-known and conspicuous bird in the areas where it occurs, frequently associating with man. With its large size, long tail and black and white plumage, there will be no problem over its identification. The population in Arabia differs in having a larger bill, dull black plumage, and small amount of white on wings and shoulders. Inhabits bushy or open country with tall trees, in which it builds a dome-shaped nest of sticks. A resident of Turkey, Cyprus and Syria, with a small, isolated population in south-west Saudi Arabia; in Israel, however, Magpies have been recorded only twice in the past thirty years.

Alpine Chough *Pyrrhocorax graculus* 38cm

A flock of crow-sized black birds with broad, fingered wings, wheeling around above mountains in Turkey, will be either Choughs (*Pyrrhocorax pyrrhocorax*) or Alpine Choughs. The Chough (not illustrated) has a long, blood-red bill, while Alpine Chough has a short, yellow bill. Both are gregarious and agile fliers, breeding at high elevations and feeding largely in mountain pastures. Their calls are characteristic: a loud, hollow, far-carrying *chow*. In Israel the Alpine Chough is a regular winter visitor to the north, but the Chough is extremely rare.

House Crow *Corvus splendens* 43cm

Look for this dark grey and black crow in coastal areas of Arabia, especially around ports. It superficially resembles the Hooded Crow (which does not occur in Arabia), but the grey is darker and the back is black; it is also slightly smaller and slimmer, with a long, deep bill and domed crown. Does not occur naturally in the Middle East, the colonies being the result of introductions from India in the last 30 years, the birds probably having arrived on grain boats. In Israel, it can be found mainly in the Eilat region.

123

Brown-necked Raven *Corvus ruficollis* 50cm

A large black bird, very similar to the Raven (*Corvus corax*), but the two are largely geographically isolated, Israel being one of the few countries where both occur: the Raven in the north and the desert-loving Brown-necked Raven in the south. The Brown-necked can be told from Raven by its slimmer wings, longer bill and bronzy-brown sheen on hindneck, but this colour can be difficult to see. When perched, note the longer wings of the Brown-necked, reaching the tail-tip. A widespread breeding bird of southern Israel, Jordan and throughout Arabia.

Fan-tailed Raven *Corvus rhipidurus* 47cm

Richard Porter

Slightly smaller and chunkier than the Brown-necked Raven, with stout bill. It is most easily recognized by its short tail: in flight, when soaring, can look almost tailless as the fanned tail merges into the hindwing. Like the Brown-necked, a bird of semi-deserts, cliffs and crags, often near human habitation and especially rubbish dumps. Resident in southern Israel, west Jordan and western and southern Arabia, from sea level to 3000m.

124

Hooded Crow *Corvus corone cornix* 47cm

A grey and black crow, the body being grey and the head and throat black, with black wings and tail. Nests solitarily, but outside the breeding season often forms large roosts at night along with Jackdaws (*Corvus monedula*), a smaller black crow with a grey hindneck and pale eye that is common in Turkey. The Hooded Crow occurs in open country with scattered trees, where it builds a large nest of sticks high in a tree or on a pylon. A resident in northern and central Israel, neighbouring Middle East countries, Turkey and Cyprus.

Tristram's Grackle *Onychognathus tristramii* 25cm

Grackles are members of the starling family. Larger than Starling, and with a glossy black plumage and orange wing patches in flight. The female is duller, with a greyish-brown head. A noisy bird, often gathering in flocks to feed on fruits. The far-carrying call resembles a wolf-whistle. Nests mostly in crevices on rock faces. The world range of this grackle is confined to the Middle East, where it is a resident of Israel, southern Jordan and western and southern Arabia, occurring from sea level to 3000m.

125

Starling *Sturnus vulgaris* 22cm

In breeding season, blackish with purple and green gloss and yellow bill. In winter, has extensive pale spots (tips to the feathers) over entire plumage. The young birds (until the early autumn) are dull brownish-grey with a black bill. A familiar bird throughout its breeding range, and in autumn and winter often in large flocks which roost communally, sometimes in tens of thousands. It occurs in a range of habitats, but particularly in or near towns and villages, where it nests in holes or crevices. In the Middle East, breeds in Turkey; in winter, numbers are swelled by migrants from the north, and birds will then occur throughout much of the region, including Israel, where abundant.

Rose-coloured Starling *Sturnus roseus* 22cm

Richard Porter

Has the structure of Starling, but is quite different in plumage with its pink body and black (with purple and green gloss) head, wings and tail. On migration, can occur in large flocks. Young birds are pale grey-brown, with orange legs and yellowish bill. In the Middle East, breeds irregularly in isolated colonies in Turkey, to which it is a summer visitor from the east; in Israel it is an uncommon migrant, as it is in most neighbouring countries of the east Mediterranean.

House Sparrow *Passer domesticus* 15cm

A familiar bird in many towns and villages in the Middle East, nesting in holes in buildings or similar crevices. Male and female differ: note the male's black bib, white cheeks, grey crown and reddish-brown hindneck, and the female's rather plain greyish-brown coloration with pale stripe above the eye and dark stripes on back and wings. The Tree Sparrow (*Passer montanus*), which is very rare in Israel, differs from the House Sparrow in its red-brown cap and black spot on white cheek. Widespread resident breeder, occurring in areas of habitation and cultivation throughout Israel and most of the region.

Spanish Sparrow *Passer hispaniolensis* 15cm

Similar to the House Sparrow, but the male is quite distinct with its chestnut crown and heavy black streakings on back and underparts. This pattern is far less obvious in the winter. Female almost impossible to tell from the female House Sparrow. Breeds colonially, often in large numbers, building a domed nest with side entrance hole in a tall tree or even the base of a White Stork's nest. Outside breeding season, will roost in big flocks. Breeds throughout Israel and neighbouring Middle East countries, including Turkey and Cyprus; occurs more widely in winter.

(Above) male; (below) female

Dead Sea Sparrow *Passer moabiticus* 12cm

(Above) male; (below) female

A small, rather colourful sparrow whose world distribution is confined to the Middle East. Note the male's small black bib and eye-stripe, both of which have a yellowish border, and the chestnut wing patch. The female is less distinct, being essentially a smaller version of a female House Sparrow. The call, a fairly high *tereep*, resembles that of the House Sparrow but is more musical. Breeds in isolated colonies, usually near water, especially rivers with adjacent tamarisks and reeds, in Israel, Iraq, Syria, Jordan, southern Turkey and Cyprus (rare).

Pale Rock Sparrow *Petronia brachydactyla* 14cm

Richard Porter

A rather featureless, sparrow-sized bird with long wings and longer, more curved bill than House Sparrow. The grey-brown plumage is relieved by darker brown wings with two paler wingbars and a whitish panel on the flight feathers. Quite different from the Rock Sparrow, which see. In the Middle East, it is a summer visitor to rocky and scrubby breeding habitats in northern Israel (Mount Hermon), Jordan and south-east Turkey; on migration, occurs rather unpredictably throughout the region, including Israel, sometimes in large flocks which resemble migrating larks.

Rock Sparrow *Petronia petronia* 14cm

A rather chunky sparrow-type with broad dark and pale stripes on crown, dark streaks on underparts, and short tail with pale spots on feather tips, these noticeable in flight. The male has a small yellow spot on the throat which is usually visible only during courtship display. Told from other sparrows by its streaked head and pale tip to tail. Does not usually occur in flocks. In the Middle East, it is a resident of high rocky areas in northern Israel, neighbouring east Mediterranean countries and much of Turkey; also found around ruins and disused buildings.

Chaffinch *Fringilla coelebs* 15cm

The male Chaffinch is a smart bird with its buff-orange underparts, grey crown and nape, and white shoulder patch, wingbar and outer tail feathers. The female is much duller, rather brownish, but also shows the white wing and tail markings of the male. Mostly ground-dwelling when feeding, and in winter often gathers in large flocks with other finches and buntings to feed in cultivated fields. In the Middle East, it breeds in woodland in Turkey and Cyprus, but in winter it migrates south to reach Israel and neighbouring countries in large numbers.

(Above) male; (below) female

Red-fronted Serin *Serinus pusillus* 12cm

Tim Loseby

A small, delightful, dark finch, the sexes of which are similar: sooty head, developing into black streaks on the back and underparts. When it turns to face you, there is a real jewel in the crown: an almost luminous orange forehead. Often in flocks, and will associate with other finches feeding on plant seeds in winter. In the Middle East, it is a resident of mountains in Turkey, occurring in junipers, conifers and birches, also neighbouring meadows; occasionally wanders south to Israel and Cyprus in winter.

European Serin *Serinus serinus* 12cm

Another small finch with a stubby bill, occurring in pairs or small flocks. The male is told by its canary-yellow face and breast and bold dark streaks on its flanks; in flight, note the yellow rump. Females are much duller, showing barely any yellow except on the rump. One of the best identification features is the call: a fast, trilling *tirrililit*. Song is musical, fast, jingling, often in bat-like flight. A bird of parks, orchards and woodland edges and, in winter, neighbouring fields and wasteland. In the Middle East, it is mainly resident in Turkey, Cyprus, western Israel and Jordan, but larger numbers occur in Israel and the east Mediterranean in winter.

Syrian Serin *Serinus syriacus* 12cm

This serin is found only in the Middle East. It resembles the European Serin, but has a longer tail and a paler plumage without any streaks on the underparts; the plain upperparts have a rather greyish hue. In summer, the male has a rich yellow forehead and throat. Sociable, often in small flocks. Breeds colonially in mountain regions with cedars and junipers in isolated areas in northern Israel (Mount Hermon region), Jordan, Lebanon and Syria; in winter, moves to lower altitudes and may be found throughout Israel, but uncommon.

Greenfinch *Carduelis chloris* 15cm

A large finch, dull yellowish-green in coloration (female browner), with distinctive yellow wing and tail patches. The stout bill is flesh-pink. The song is a musical twittering, often uttered in bat-like display flight. Semi-colonial in the breeding season, but often in flocks with other seed-eaters in winter. Occurs in farmland, plantations, parks and oases, nesting in a low tree. In the Middle East, a resident of northern and central Israel and neighbouring east Mediterranean countries, including Turkey and Cyprus; some immigration from the north in winter.

Goldfinch *Carduelis carduelis* 12cm

One of the most distinctive birds in Israel and the northern part of the Middle East (does not occur in the south). Easily told by its red face, black and white head pattern, and black wings with conspicuous broad yellow wingbar, especially noticeable in flight. Note, too, the 'dancing' flight and tinkling liquid flight call. Often seen in small groups feeding on thistles. A bird of orchards, gardens, farmland with trees and waste ground. Mainly resident in Turkey, Cyprus and the countries bordering the Mediterranean.

Linnet *Carduelis cannabina* 14cm

A sprightly finch, the male of which is easily identified in the breeding season by its red forehead, two red breast patches, chestnut back, and white wing-flashes when it flies. At other times of the year, the male resembles the female and young birds, being dull greyish-brown with streaked breast; but in all ages and plumages shows the white wing-flashes in flight. Occurs in open country with trees and scrub, where often seen in small flocks. Breeds semi-colonially in Israel, other parts of the east Mediterranean and Turkey, areas to which it is also a winter visitor.

132

Desert Finch *Rhodospiza obsoleta* 15cm

Rather inaptly named, as it does not occur in deserts but in dry open country with trees, orchards and vineyards. About the size of a Greenfinch, this greyish-buff finch is easily told by its prominent black bill, black face-mask (on male only), and black, white and pink wing pattern, especially noticeable in flight. In the breeding season usually seen in pairs, but in winter flocks can gather in cultivated fields. Breeds in southern Israel, Jordan, south-east Turkey and north Arabia.

Trumpeter Finch *Bucanetes githagineus* 13cm

A rather inconspicuous, ground-dwelling finch with large head, short tail and stout bill. The male in breeding plumage has an orange-red bill, and grey-buff plumage with a pinkish wash on underparts, wings and forehead. Females and juveniles are simply sandy grey-buff with yellowish-brown bill. Note that, in all plumages, the legs are orange-coloured.

(Above) male; (below) female

Its song – a drawn out nasal buzzing – gives rise to the name of Trumpeter Finch. Occurs on rather barren, rocky hillsides and plains. A breeding resident of southern Israel and, patchily, throughout the Middle East.

Common Rosefinch *Carpodacus erythrinus* 14cm

Dennis Green; Windrush Photos

The female and juvenile are drab brownish finches with a stout bill, well-streaked underparts and two pale wingbars. The adult male, with its red crown, face and breast, is more likely to be recognized. A semi-colonial breeder, and often the song is the first indication of its presence: a clear whistle in three parts, *wheety-wheety-wee*. Occurs in wooded mountains, usually near streams and wet valley bottoms. A summer visitor to its breeding grounds in northern Turkey; on migration, rather scarce in Israel and neighbouring east Mediterranean countries.

Sinai Rosefinch *Carpodacus synoicus* 14cm

(Above) male; (below) female

One of the Middle East's specialities, and the national bird of Jordan. The male is easily told by its crimson-pink plumage, with frosty streaking on crown and ear-coverts; the upperparts are grey-brown with a mauve tinge. Females and juveniles are a drab grey-buff with faint streaking, and with a gingery wash to the face; like the male they show no wingbars in rather bounding flight. Rather nervous behaviour and often in groups, especially in winter. Its breeding range is confined to a small area of southern Israel and southern Jordan, where it occurs in barren, rocky hills.

Hawfinch *Coccothraustes coccothraustes* 18cm

Tim Loseby

A large, robust finch with powerful bill, which is lead-grey in summer and pale in winter. Note its short tail with white tip, white shoulder patches and, in flight, white stripe through flight feathers. A rather secretive bird of deciduous forests and orchards, but often in small groups, especially on migration. In the Middle East, breeds only in a few areas of western Turkey; in autumn, birds from Europe migrate into the region for the winter and some reach Israel and neighbouring countries, where, in some years, they can be quite common.

Pine Bunting *Emberiza leucocephalos* 16cm

In shape and behaviour very similar to Yellowhammer (*Emberiza citrinella*), which is very familiar in much of Europe but a scarce winter visitor to Israel. The male Pine Bunting is a mixture of chestnut, grey and white, the head pattern being quite distinct, with chestnut throat bordered below by white neck-band and above by white patch behind the eye. Female and immature like Yellowhammer but with the yellow colour replaced by white. Occurs in farmland, woodland edges and similar habitats. A scarce winter visitor to Israel and a vagrant elsewhere in the Middle East.

Rock Bunting *Emberiza cia* 16cm

The grey head with black stripes makes the male Rock Bunting striking; in addition, note its rusty-coloured body. The female is less distinctive, showing just a shadow of the male's richer plumage. In flight, both show a rusty rump and white outer tail feathers. The most characteristic call is a thin *tsip*, often heard before the bird is located. A resident of rocky and scrubby mountains in northern Israel, which is the southern limit of its range in the Middle East.

House Bunting *Emberiza striolata* 14cm

Superficially resembles a small, dull Rock Bunting, but told by its orange lower mandible, rufous upperparts, more finely streaked dull grey crown and throat, and rufous (not white) outer tail feathers. The female is duller, with an even more diffuse head pattern. A resident of rather desolate rocky and sandy wadis with little vegetation, nesting in hole or crevice in rock face or building. It breeds in the southern half of Israel and patchily elsewhere in the Middle East; where it does occur, it can be quite common.

Cineraous Bunting *Emberiza cineracea* 17cm

A rather rare, nondescript bunting whose distribution is confined to the Middle East. The male has a greenish-yellow wash to the head, but is otherwise greyish; the female is darker and even duller, heavily streaked, and with a yellowish-green tinge on the throat. Differs further from Ortolan and Cretzschmar's Buntings in greyish (not pinkish) bill. A summer visitor to dry, rocky areas, mainly in southern Turkey, up to the treeline. Its migration through the region is little known, but in Israel it is frequent in spring and less so in autumn.

Ortolan Bunting *Emberiza hortulana* 17cm

The male has a green-grey head and upper breast, yellow moustache and throat, streaked upperparts and chestnut underparts. Note particularly the pale eye-ring. The female is much more drab, with finely streaked crown and upper breast, and is best separated from other buntings by its yellowish moustache and eye-ring. A largely ground-dwelling bunting which occurs in small flocks on migration. A summer visitor to its Middle East breeding grounds in Turkey; widespread on passage throughout the region, including Israel, where it is common, especially in spring.

137

Cretzschmar's Bunting *Emberiza caesia* 15cm

(Above) male; (below) female

Resembles Ortolan Bunting, but with a blue-grey head and the yellow on the face replaced by orange. The female is like a drab version of the male, and young birds are very like Ortolans but with a more rusty hue. Frequently first located by its simple but often repeated three- or four-note song: *dsi-dsi-dsi dsiu*, the last note slightly lower. A bird of rocky hillsides, usually with scattered bushes, but on migration will inhabit farmland and desert fringes. A summer visitor to Israel (which is at the southern limit of its small world range), the east Mediterranean, southern Turkey and Cyprus.

Reed Bunting *Emberiza schoeniclus* 16cm

Alan Williams

The male is easily told by its black head and bib, white moustache and collar, and reedbed habitat. The female is streaked brownish, with pale stripe above the eye, and with broad whitish moustache bordered by a black streak above and below. In the Middle East, Reed Buntings are breeding residents in scattered wetlands with reedbeds in Turkey; in winter, more northerly populations migrate south into the region, and they can then be quite common in reedy areas in Israel.

Black-headed Bunting *Emberiza melanocephala* 17cm

There can be no mistaking the male with its yellow underparts, black head and chestnut back. The female and immature birds are less distinctive, with grey-brown upperparts and pale yellowish underparts, including the undertail-coverts. Unlike most buntings, both sexes at all ages have dark outer tail feathers. The males sing repeatedly from a prominent perch in open scrub or agricultural country with hedgerows and small trees. A summer visitor from its eastern wintering area to Middle East breeding grounds that extend from northern Israel north to Turkey and Cyprus; also occurs on migration in northern Arabia, but generally rather scarce.

Corn Bunting *Miliaria calandra* 18cm

A stout, rather drab bunting with thick pale yellowish bill and streaked plumage; shows a broad buffish band above the eye. The sexes are similar, but the male characteristically dangles its legs when flying between songposts. The monotonous song is rather like the jangling of a set of keys. Occurs in cultivation, mountain steppes and meadows. Largely resident in its Middle East breeding grounds in northern Israel, the east Mediterranean, Turkey and Cyprus; more widespread in winter, when migrants arrive from Europe and Asia.

Further reading

If this book has whetted your appetite, then you will want to learn more about the birds of Israel and the Middle East. The four most useful books are:

Shirihai, Hadoram. *The Birds of Israel*. Academic Press, London, 1996.

Porter, R.F., S. Christensen and P. Schiermacker-Hansen. *Field Guide to the Birds of the Middle East*. T & AD Poyser, London, 1996.

Mullarney, K., Svensson, L., Zetterstrom, D. and Grant, P.J. *Collins Bird Guide*. Harper Collins, London, 1999

Evans, M.I. *Important Bird Areas in the Middle East*. BirdLife International, Cambridge, U.K., 1994. (This contains a chapter on Israel.)

There is also a very useful set of sound recordings on two tapes:

Mild, K. *Bird Songs of Israel and the Middle East*.

Index

Accentor, Black-
    throated 92
    Radde's 92
Accipiter brevipes 35
    nisus 35
*Acrocephalus
    arundinaceus* 104
    melanopogon 103
    palustris 104
    schoenobaenus 103
    scirpaceus 104
    stentoreus 104
Actitis hypoleucos 59
Aegypius monachus 33
Alaemon alaudipes 83
Alauda arvensis 82, 84
Alcedo atthis 77
Alectoris chukar 42
Ammomanes cincturus
    82
    deserti 82
Ammoperdix heyi 42
Anas acuta 27
    clypeata 28
    crecca 28
    penelope 27
    platyrhynchos 27
    querquedula 28
Anser albifrons 26
    anser 26
Anthropoides virgo 45
Anthus campestris 87
    cervinus 88
    pratensis 88
    richardi 87
    similis 88
    trivialis 88
Apus apus 76
    melba 76
    pallidus 76
Aquila chrysaetos 38
    clanga 37
    heliaca 38
    nipalensis 37
    pomarina 36
Ardea cinerea 22
    purpurea 22
Athene noctua 74
Avocet 47
Aythya fuligula 30
Aythya nyroca 30

Babbler, Arabian 115
Bee-eater, Blue-
    cheeked 79
    European 79
    Little Green 78
Bittern, Little 19
Blackbird 101
Blackcap 111
Blackstart 96
Bluethroat 94

Booby, Brown 17
Bubo bubo 73
Bubulcus ibis 20
Bucanetes githagineus
    133
Bulbul, Yellow-vented
    91
Bunting, Black-headed
    139
    Cinereous 137
    Corn 139
    Cretzschmar's 138
    House 136
    Ortolan 137
    Pine 135
    Reed 138
    Rock 136
Burhinus capensis 48
    oedicnemus 48
    senegalensis 48
Bustard, Houbara 46
Buteo buteo 35
    rufinus 36
Butorides striatus 20
Buzzard, Common 35
    Honey 35
    Long-legged 36

*Calandrella
    brachydactyla* 84
Calidris alpina 53–54
    ferruginea 53
    minuta 53
    temminckii 53
Calonectris diomedea 15
Caprimulgus aegyptius
    75
    europaeus 75
    nubicus 75
Carduelis cannabina
    132
    carduelis 132
    chloris 131
Carpodacus erythrinus
    134
    synoicus 134
Cercomela melanura 96
Cercotrichas galactotes
    93
    podobe 93
Ceryle rudis 78
Chaffinch 129
*Charadrius
    alexandrinus* 50
    asiaticus 51
    dubius 49
    hiaticula 49–50
    leschenaultii 50
    mongolus 50
Chettusia gregaria 52
    leucura 52
Chiffchaff 113

Chlamydotis undulata
    46
Chlidonias hybridus 66
    leucopterus 66
    niger 66
Chough 123
    Alpine 123
Chukar 42
Ciconia ciconia 23
    nigra 23
Circaetus gallicus 33
Circus aeruginosus 34
    macrourus 34
    pygargus 34
Cisticola, Fan-tailed
    101
Cisticola juncidis 101
Clamator glandarius 72
*Coccothraustes
    coccothraustes* 135
Columba livia 69
    oenas 69
Coot 45
Coracias garrulus 80
Cormorant, Great 17
    Pygmy 17
Corvus corax 124
    corone cornix 125
    monedula 125
    rhipidurus 124
    ruficollis 124
    splendens 123
Coturnix coturnix 43
Courser, Cream-
    coloured 48
Crake, Baillon's 44
    Little 43–44
    Spotted 43
Crane, Common 45
    Demoiselle 45
Crow, Hooded 125
    House 123
Cuckoo, Common 72
    Great Spotted 72
Cuculus canorus 72
Curlew 56
    Slender-billed 56
Cursorius cursor 48

Dendrocopos major 81
    syriacus 81
Dove, African
    Collared 69
    Collared 69
    Laughing 70
    Namaqua 71
    Rock 69
    Stock 69
    Turtle 70
Duck, Ferruginous 30
    Tufted 30
    White-headed 30

141

Dunlin 53–54
Dunnock 92

Eagle, Bonelli's 38
  Golden 38
  Greater Spotted 37
  Imperial 38
  Lesser Spotted 36
  Short-toed 33
  Steppe 37
Egret, Cattle 20
  Great White 22
  Little 21
Egretta alba 22
  garzetta 21
  gularis 21
Emberiza caesia 138
  cia 136
  cineracea 137
  citrinella 135
  hortulana 137
  leucocephalos 135
  melanocephala 139
  schoeniclus 138
  striolata 136
Eremophila alpestris 85
  bilopha 85

Falco concolor 41
  naumanni 39
  pelegrinoides 41
  peregrinus 41
  subbuteo 40
  tinnunculus 39
  vespertinus 40
Falcon, Barbary 41
  Peregrine 41
  Red-footed 40
  Sooty 41
Ficedula albicollis 114
  hypoleuca 114
  parva 114
  semitorquata 114
Finch, Desert 133
  Trumpeter 133
Flamingo, Greater 25
Flycatcher, Collared
    114
  Pied 114
  Red-breasted 114
  Semi-collared 114
  Spotted 113
Fringilla coelebs 129
Fulica atra 45

Galerida cristata 84
Gallinago gallinago 55
  media 55
Gallinula chloropus 45
Gallinule, Purple 44
Garganey 28
Garrulus glandarius
    122
Gelochelidon nilotica 63

Geronticus eremita 24
Glareola nordmanni 49
  pratincola 49
Godwit, Bar-tailed 55
  Black-tailed 55
Goldfinch 132
Goose, Greylag 26
  White-fronted 26
Grackle, Tristram's
    125
Grebe, Black-necked
    15
  Great Crested 14
Greenfinch 131
Greenshank 57
Grus grus 45
Gull, Black-headed
    62
  Caspian 63
  Great Black-headed
    61
  Lesser Black-backed
    62
  Mediterranean 61
  Sooty 60
  White-eyed 60
  Yellow-legged 63
Gypaetus barbatus 32
Gyps fulvus 33

Halcyon smyrnensis 77
Harrier, Marsh 34
  Montagu's 34
  Pallid 34
Hawfinch 135
Heron, Grey 22
  Night 19
  Purple 22
  Striated 20
  Western Reef 21
Hieraaetus fasciatus 38
Himantopus himantopus
    47
Hippolais languida 105
  olivetorum 106
  pallida 105
Hirundo daurica 87
  rustica 86
Hobby 40
Hoopoe 80
Hoplopterus indicus 52
  spinosus 52
Hypocolius, Grey 91
Hypocolius ampelinus
    91

Ibis, Bald 24
  Glossy 24
Irania gutturalis 95
Ixobrychus minutus 19

Jackdaw 125
Jay 122
Jynx torquilla 81

Kestrel, Common 39
  Lesser 39
Kingfisher, Common
    77
  Pied 78
  White-breasted 77
Kite, Black 31
  Red 31

Lammergeier 32
Lanius collurio 119
  excubitor 120
  isabellinus 119
  meridionalis 120
  minor 120
  nubicus 121
  senator 121
Lapwing 52
Lark, Bar-tailed
    Desert 82
  Bimaculated 83
  Calandra 83
  Crested 84
  Desert 82
  Hoopoe 83
  Shore 85
  Short-toed 84
  Temminck's
    Horned 85
Larus cachinnans 63
  fuscus 62
  hemprichii 60
  ichthyaetus 61
  leucophthalmus 60
  melanocephalus 61
  michahellis 63
  ridibundus 62
Limicola falcinellus 54
Limosa lapponica 55
  limosa 55
Linnet 132
Luscinia luscinia 94
  megarhynchos 94
  svecica 94
Lymnocryptes minimus
    55

Magpie 122
Mallard 27
Marmaronetta
    angustirostris 29
Martin, African Rock
    86
  Crag 86
  Sand 85
Melanocorypha
    bimaculata 83
  calandra 83
Merops apiaster 79
  orientalis 78
  superciliosus 79
Miliaria calandra 139
Milvus migrans 31
  milvus 31

Monticola saxatilis 100
  solitarius 100
Moorhen 45
Motacilla alba 90
  cinerea 90
  citreola 89
  flava 89
Muscicapa striata 113

Nectarinia osea 118
Neophron percnopterus 32
Netta rufina 29
Nightingale, Common 94
  Thrush 94
Nightjar, Egyptian 75
  European 75
  Nubian 75
Numenius arquata 56
  phaeopus 56
  tenuirostris 56
Nuthatch, Eastern Rock 116
  Great Rock 116
  Western Rock 116
Nycticorax nycticorax 19

Oena capensis 71
Oenanthe bottae 97
  cypriaca 97
  deserti 98
  hispanica 98
  isabellina 98
  leucopyga 99
  monacha 99
  oenanthe 97
  pleschanka 97
Onychognathus tristramii 125
Oriole, Golden 118
Oriolus oriolus 118
Osprey 39
Ostrich 14
Otus brucei 73
  scops 73
  senegalensis 73
Owl, African Scops 73
  Eagle 73
  European Scops 73
  Hume's Tawny 74
  Little 74
  Striated Scops 73
  Tawny 74
Oxyura leucocephala 30

Pandion haliaetus 39
Parakeet, Ring-necked 71
Partridge, Sand 42
Parus lugubris 115
  major 116

Passer domesticus 127
  hispaniolensis 127
  moabiticus 128
  montanus 127
Pelecanus crispus 18
  onocrotalus 18
  rufescens 18
Pelican, Dalmatian 18
  Pink-backed 18
  White 18
Pernis apivorus 31
Petronia brachydactyla 128
  petronia 129
Phaethon aethereus 16
Phalacrocorax carbo 17
  pygmeus 17
Phalarope Red-necked 59
Phalaropus lobatus 59
Philomachus pugnax 54
Phoenicopterus ruber 25
Phoenicurus ochruros 95
  phoenicurus 95
Phylloscopus collybita 113
  orientalis 112
  trochilus 112
Pica pica 122
Pintail 27
Pipit, Long-billed 88
  Meadow 88
  Red-throated 88
  Richard's 87
  Tawny 87
  Tree 88
Platalea leucorodia 25
Plegadis falcinellus 24
Plover, Caspian 51
  European Golden 51–52
  Greater Sand 50
  Grey 51
  Kentish 50
  Lesser Sand 50
  Little Ringed 49
  Pacific Golden 51
  Red-wattled 52
  Ringed 49–50
  Sociable 52
  Spur-winged 52
  White-tailed 52
Pluvialis apricaria 51–52
  fulva 51
  squatarola 51
Pochard, Red-crested 29
Podiceps cristatus 14
  nigricollis 15
Porphyrio porphyrio 44
Porzana parva 43–44
  porzana 43
  pusilla 44

Pratincole, Black-winged 49
  Collared 49
Prinia, Graceful 102
Prinia gracilis 102
Prunella atrogularis 92
  modularis 92
  ocularis 92
Psittacula krameri 71
Pterocles alchata 68
  coronatus 67
  lichtensteinii 67
  orientalis 68
  senegallus 67–68
Ptyonoprogne fuligula 86
  rupestris 86
Puffinus yelkouan 16
Pycnonotus xanthopygos 91
Pyrrhocorax graculus 123
  pyrrhocorax 123

Quail 43

Raven 124
  Brown-necked 124
  Fan-tailed 124
Recurvirostra avosetta 47
Redshank 57
Redstart, Black 95
  Common 95
Remiz pendulinus 117
Rhodospiza obsoleta 133
Riparia riparia 85
Robin, Black Bush 93
  Rufous Bush 93
  White-throated 95
Roller, European 80
Rosefinch, Common 134
  Sinai 134
Rostratula benghalensis 46
Ruff 54

Sandgrouse, Black-bellied 68
  Crowned 67
  Lichtenstein's 67
  Pin-tailed 68
  Spotted 67–68
Sandpiper, Broad-billed 54
  Common 59
  Curlew 53
  Green 58
  Marsh 57
  Terek 58
  Wood 58

143

Saxicola torquata 96
Scotocerca inquieta 102
Serin, European 130
  Red-fronted 130
  Syrian 131
Serinus pusillus 130
  serinus 130
  syriacus 131
Shearwater, Cory's 15
  Mediterranean 16
Shelduck, Ruddy 26
Shoveler 28
Shrike, Great Grey
  120
  Isabelline 119
  Lesser Grey 120
  Masked 121
  Red-backed 119
  Southern Grey 120
  Woodchat 121
Sitta neumayer 116
  tephronota 116
Skylark 82, 84
Snipe, Common 55
Snipe, Great 55
Snipe, Jack 55
Snipe, Painted 46
Sparrow, Dead Sea
  128
  House 127
  Pale Rock 128
  Rock 129
  Spanish 127
  Tree 127
Sparrowhawk,
  Eurasian 35
  Levant 35
Spoonbill 25
Starling 126
  Rose-coloured 126
Sterna albifrons 65
  bengalensis 64
  bergii 64
  caspia 64
  hirundo 65
  sandvicensis 64
  saundersi 65
Stilt, Black-winged 47
Stint, Little 53
  Temminck's 53
Stone-curlew 48
Stonechat 96
Stork, Black 23
  White 23
Streptopelia decaocto 69
  roseogrisea 69
  senegalensis 70
  turtur 70
Strix aluco 74
  butleri 74

Struthio camelus 14
Sturnus roseus 126
  vulgaris 126
Sula leucogaster 17
Sunbird, Palestine
  118
Swallow, Barn 86
  Red-rumped 87
Swift, Alpine 76
  Common 76
  Pallid 76
Sylvia atricapilla 111
  borin 111
  cantillans 107
  communis 111
  conspicillata 106
  curruca 110
  hortensis 109
  leucomelaena 109
  melanocephala 108
  melanothorax 108
  mystacea 107
  nisoria 110
  rueppelli 109

Tadorna ferruginea 26
Teal 28
  Marbled 29
Tern, Black 66
  Caspian 64
  Common 65
  Gull-billed 63
  Lesser Crested 64
  Little 65
  Sandwich 64
  Saunders's 65
  Swift 64
  Whiskered 66
  White-winged Black
  66
Thick-knee, Senegal
  48
  Spotted 48
Thrush, Blue Rock
  100
  Rock 100
Tichodroma muraria
  117
Tit, Great 116
  Penduline 117
  Sombre 115
Tringa glareola 58
  nebularia 57
  ochropus 58
  stagnatilis 57
  totanus 57
Tropicbird, Red-billed
  16
Turdoides squamiceps
  115
Turdus merula 101

Upupa epops 80

Vanellus vanellus 52
Vulture, Black 33
  Egyptian 32
  Griffon 33

Wagtail, Citrine 89
  Grey 90
  White 90
  Yellow 89
Wallcreeper 117
Warbler, Arabian 109
  Barred 110
  Eastern Bonelli's
  112
  Clamorous Reed
  104
  Cyprus 108
  European Reed 104
  Garden 111
  Great Reed 104
  Marsh 104
  Ménétries's 107
  Moustached 103
  Olivaceous 105
  Olive-tree 106
  Orphean 109
  Rüppell's 109
  Sardinian 108
  Scrub 102
  Sedge 103
  Spectacled 106
  Subalpine 107
  Upcher's 105
  Willow 112
Wheatear, Black-eared
  98
  Cyprus Pied 97
  Desert 98
  Hooded 99
  Isabelline 97
  Northern 97
  Pied 97
  Red-breasted 97
  White-crowned
  Black 99
Whimbrel 56
Whitethroat 111
  Desert Lesser 110
  Hume's Lesser 110
  Lesser 110
Wigeon 27
Woodpecker, Great
  Spotted 81
  Syrian 81
Wryneck 81

Xenus cinereus 58

Yellowhammer 135